Skills Worksheet

Directed Reading A

Section: What Is Sound?

SOUND AND VIBRATIONS

1. The complete back-and-forth motion of an object is called a(n)

_______________________.

2. In a(n) _______________________ the particles in the air are closer together than in the surrounding air.

3. In a(n) _______________________, the particles in the air are less crowded than in the surrounding air.

4. Longitudinal waves that are caused by vibrations and travel through a

medium are called _______________________.

5. As sound waves leave their source, in what direction do they travel?

____

6. Air does not travel with sound waves. But what would happen at the school dance if air did travel with sound?

____

____

7. A substance through which a wave can travel is a(n)

_______________________.

8. Why is there no sound in a vacuum?

____

9. Why does the sound of the ringing alarm clock get quieter as the air is removed?

____

____

HOW YOU DETECT SOUND

_______**10.** After your ears convert sound waves into electrical signals, where are the signals sent for interpretation?
  a. pinna
  b. spinal cord
  c. brain
  d. oval window

Copyright © by Holt, Rinehart and Winston. All rights reserved.

Directed Reading A *continued*

Match the labels to the parts of the drawing. Write the letters in the spaces provided.

_______**11.** ear canal

_______**12.** pinna

_______**13.** cochlea

_______**14.** eardrum

_______**15.** hammer

_______**16.** anvil

_______**17.** stirrup

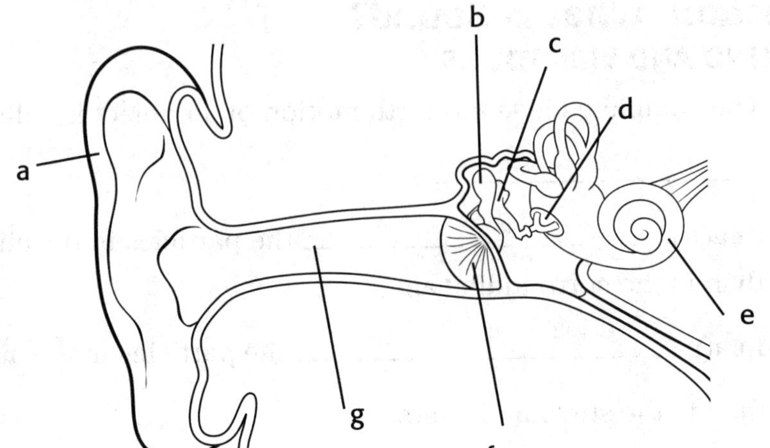

Match the labels to the parts of the drawing. Write the letters in the spaces provided.

_______**18.** middle ear

_______**19.** outer ear

_______**20.** inner ear

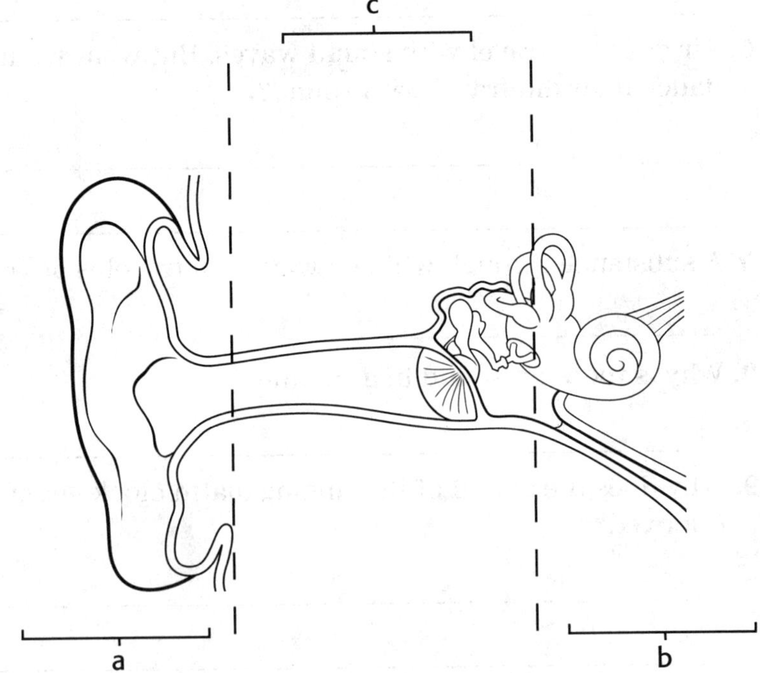

Copyright © by Holt, Rinehart and Winston. All rights reserved.

| Directed Reading A *continued*

Match the correct definition with the correct term. Write the letter in the space provided.

_______**21.** the outermost portion of the ear

_______**22.** bends to stimulate nerves

_______**23.** portion of the ear that contains liquid

_______**24.** the bone that vibrates the oval window

_______**25.** the eardrum makes this bone vibrate

a. cochlea

b. pinna

c. hammer

d. stirrup

e. hair cell

26. What happens to the surrounding air when a tree falls and hits the ground?

____

____

HEARING LOSS AND DEAFNESS

_______**27.** Loud sounds can cause damage to the
   a. hair cells and nerve endings.
   b. oval window.
   c. eardrum.
   d. hammer, anvil, and stirrup.

_______**28.** How can you protect yourself from tinnitus?
   a. Drink a glass of milk each day.
   b. Wear earplugs near loud sounds.
   c. Get lots of sleep.
   d. Turn up the radio.

Copyright © by Holt, Rinehart and Winston. All rights reserved.

Skills Worksheet

Directed Reading A

Section: Properties of Sound

1. The differences between sounds depend on the properties of the

_______________________ .

THE SPEED OF SOUND

_______ **2.** How quickly a sound reaches your ears depends on
  a. how loud or soft the sound is.
  b. the medium through which the sound is traveling.
  c. what causes the sound.
  d. the properties of the sound.

3. In general, what happens to the speed of sound as a medium cools?

____

____

4. What happens to particles as they slow down?

____

____

5. What did Chuck Yeager accomplish in 1947?

____

____

PITCH AND FREQUENCY

_______ **6.** A measure of how high or how low a sound is perceived to be is
  a. its pitch.   **c.** its speed.
  b. its frequency.   **d.** its medium.

_______ **7.** Pitch is NOT related to
  a. the frequency of the sound wave.
  b. the number of Hertz of the sound.
  c. the number of sound waves produced in a given time.
  d. how far away source of the sound is from your ear.

_______ **8.** The sound produced by a dog whistle
  a. has a frequency too low for people to hear.
  b. has a pitch too low for people to hear.
  c. cannot be heard by a dog.
  d. is called an ultrasonic sound.

Copyright © by Holt, Rinehart and Winston. All rights reserved.

Directed Reading A *continued*

9. The apparent change in the frequency of a sound caused by the motion of

either the listener or the source of the sound is the _______________________.

10. What happens to the sound waves from a moving source, such as a car with its horn honking, when the sound waves are moving in the same direction as the car?

____

____

11. How do the frequency and pitch of the sound seem to a person in front of a moving car with its horn honking?

____

____

12. How do the frequency and pitch of the sound seem to a person behind a moving car with its horn honking?

____

____

13. What happens to the pitch of the sound that the driver hears?

____

____

LOUDNESS AND AMPLITUDE

Match the correct definition with the correct term. Write the letter in the space provided.

_______**14.** the unit used to express how loud or soft a sound is perceived

_______**15.** how loud or soft a sound is perceived

_______**16.** the maximum distance the particles in a wave vibrate from their rest positions

a. decibel

b. loudness

c. amplitude

Copyright © by Holt, Rinehart and Winston. All rights reserved.

Directed Reading A *continued*

"SEEING" AMPLITUDE AND FREQUENCY

17. What does an oscilloscope do?

____

____

____

____

Look at the two sounds represented on the oscilloscope screens below. Then, answer the following questions.

18. How is the frequency of the sounds different?

____

____

19. How is the pitch of the sounds different?

____

____

20. What does the line on a graph from an oscilloscope represent?

____

____

Copyright © by Holt, Rinehart and Winston. All rights reserved.

Skills Worksheet

Directed Reading A

Section: Interactions of Sound Waves

REFLECTION OF SOUND WAVES

1. List two reasons why sounds are important to beluga whales.

____

____

2. The bouncing back of a wave after it strikes a barrier is called a(n)

_______________________.

3. A reflected sound wave is a(n) _______________________.

4. What kind of a surface is the best reflector of sound?

____

5. What will a shout in a gymnasium usually produce more of than a shout in an auditorium?

____

6. The use of reflected sounds by animals such as bats to find objects is called

_______________________.

7. How does the Doppler effect help bats find food?

____

8. The process of using reflected sound waves to find objects is called

_______________________.

9. What are three ways that sonar is used?

____

____

____

10. The term for a medical procedure that uses echoes to "see" inside a patient's

body is called _______________________.

11. What are three ways that ultrasonic waves can be used in medicine?

____

____

____

Copyright © by Holt, Rinehart and Winston. All rights reserved.

| **Directed Reading A** *continued*

INTERFERENCE OF SOUND WAVES

12. When two or more waves combine to form a single wave,

_____________________________ occurs.

13. In _____________________________ interference, two sound waves combine so that the compressions of one wave overlap the rarefactions of another wave to produce a softer sound.

14. In _____________________________ interference, two sound waves combine so that the compressions of one wave overlap the compressions of another wave to produce a louder sound.

15. When an airplane travels faster than the speed of sound, a(n)

_____________________________ is created.

16. Explain what happens when a jet flies at supersonic speeds.

____

____

____

17. In a(n) _____________________________, a pattern of vibration looks like a wave that is standing still.

RESONANCE

18. What is resonance?

____

____

19. Under what circumstances can a tuning fork cause a guitar string to vibrate without touching it?

____

____

20. How does a guitar use resonance to make sound?

____

____

____

Copyright © by Holt, Rinehart and Winston. All rights reserved.

Skills Worksheet

Directed Reading A

Section: Sound Quality

_______ **1.** What is the difference between music and sound?
    a. loudness   **c.** amplitude
    b. pitch   **d.** sound quality

WHAT IS SOUND QUALITY?

2. Why do the same notes sound different on different instruments?

____

____

3. The result of several pitches mixing together through interference is

_______________________.

SOUND QUALITY OF INSTRUMENTS

_______ **4.** What causes differences in sound quality among different musical instruments?
    a. interference   **c.** structural differences
    b. frequency   **d.** standing waves

Match the correct family with each instrument. Write the letter in the space provided. Each term will be used more than once.

_______ **5.** drum   **a.** string instrument

_______ **6.** guitar   **b.** wind instrument

_______ **7.** trumpet   **c.** percussion instrument

_______ **8.** cello

_______ **9.** bells

_______ **10.** tuba

_______ **11.** clarinet

_______ **12.** banjo

_______ **13.** cymbals

_______ **14.** saxophone

_______ **15.** violin

Copyright © by Holt, Rinehart and Winston. All rights reserved.

Directed Reading A *continued*

Fill in each blank in questions 16 through 18 using either *lower pitch* or *higher pitch*.

16. In a string instrument, a thicker string has a ________________________.

17. In a wind instrument, lengthening the air column produces a

________________________.

18. Among percussion instruments, larger instruments produce a

________________________.

MUSIC OR NOISE?

_______**19.** Which of the following would produce a sound wave with a repeating
pattern?
a. slamming a door   **c.** keys falling to the floor
b. French horn   **d.** truck engine

20. A sound that consists of a random mix of frequencies is a(n)

________________________.

21. What is the difference between the two sound waves shown in the
oscilloscopes below?

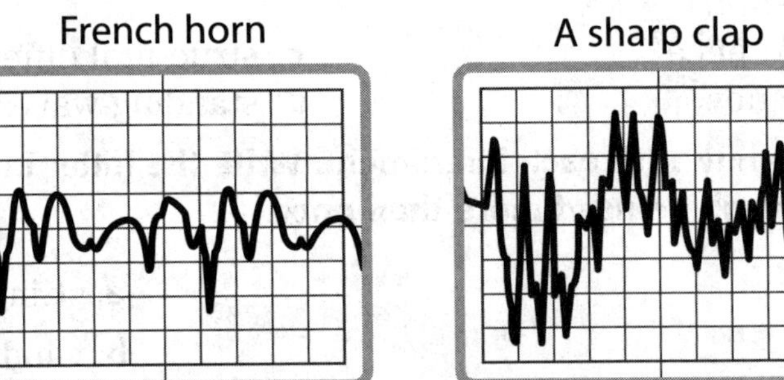

____

____

____

Copyright © by Holt, Rinehart and Winston. All rights reserved.

Skills Worksheet)

Directed Reading B

Section: What Is Sound?
SOUND AND VIBRATIONS

Read the words in the box. Read the sentences. <u>Fill in each blank</u> with the word or phrase that best completes the sentence.

rarefaction	vibration	compression

1. The complete back-and-forth motion of an object is a

_________________________.

2. In a _____________________, air particles are closer

together than in other air.

3. In a _____________________, air particles are less crowded

than in other air.

Sound Waves

sound wave	in all directions

4. A longitudinal wave caused by the back and forth motion of matter

is called a(n) _____________________.

5. Sound waves travel _____________________ away from

where they started.

Copyright © by Holt, Rinehart and Winston. All rights reserved.

Directed Reading B *continued*

Circle the letter of the best answer for each question.

6. Air does not travel with sound waves. If it did, what would happen at the school dance?

a. You couldn't hear the music.

b. The sound would not move.

c. A strong wind would blow.

d. The music would sound louder.

Sound and Media

Read the words in the box. Read the sentences. Fill in each blank with the word or phrase that best completes the sentence.

vacuum	medium

7. A substance through which a wave can travel is called a

_______________________________.

8. There are no bits of matter to vibrate in a

_______________________________.

HOW YOU DETECT SOUND

Circle the letter of the best answer for each question.

9. Where do electrical signals from the inner ear travel to?

a. outer ear

b. brain

c. eardrum

d. middle ear

Copyright © by Holt, Rinehart and Winston. All rights reserved.

Directed Reading B *continued*

Read the description. Then, <u>draw a line</u> from the dot to the matching word.

10. part of the outer ear   ●

a. hammer, anvil, and stirrup

11. part of the middle ear   ●

b. eardrum

12. part of the inner ear   ●

c. pinna

13. flap of skin found at the   ● end of the ear canal

d. cochlea

<u>Circle the letter</u> of the best answer for each question.

14. Where does the pinna direct sound to?

   a. the eardrum

   b. the ear canal

   c. the oval window

   d. the cochlea

15. Where does the size of the vibrations get bigger?

   a. in the outer ear

   b. in the middle ear

   c. in the inner ear

   d. in the brain

16. What part of the ear bends?

   a. the cochlea

   b. the oval window

   c. the anvil

   d. the hair cells

Copyright © by Holt, Rinehart and Winston. All rights reserved.

Circle the letter of the best answer for each question.

17. What part of the ear contains liquid?

    a. cochlea   **c.** hammer

    b. pinna   **d.** stirrup

18. What bone vibrates the oval window?

    a. cochlea

    b. pinna

    c. hammer

    d. stirrup

Making Sound Versus Hearing Sound

19. What forms in the air when a tree falls to the ground?

    a. nothing

    b. compressions and rarefactions

    c. electrical signals

    d. a riddle

HEARING LOSS AND DEAFNESS

20. What can loud sounds damage?

    a. hair cells and nerve endings

    b. oval window

    c. eardrum

    d. hammer, anvil, and stirrup

Protecting Your Hearing

21. How can you protect your ears?

    a. Drink milk each day.

    b. Wear earplugs.

    c. Get lots of sleep.

    d. Turn up the radio.

Copyright © by Holt, Rinehart and Winston. All rights reserved.

Skills Worksheet

Directed Reading B

Section: Properties of Sound

Circle the letter of the best answer for each question.

1. What causes differences between sounds?

   a. properties of sound waves

   b. speed of sound waves

   c. temperature of sound waves

   d. person hearing sound

THE SPEED OF SOUND

2. What affects how fast a sound reaches your ears?

   a. its loudness or softness

   b. the medium

   c. what causes the sound

   d. the properties of the sound

How the Speed of Sound Can Change

3. What happens to the speed of sound as a medium cools?

   a. speeds up

   b. slows down

   c. stays the same

   d. speeds up and then slows

4. What happens to particles as they slow down?

   a. pass on energy faster

   b. pass on energy more slowly

   c. get warmer

   d. get colder

Copyright © by Holt, Rinehart and Winston. All rights reserved.

Directed Reading B *continued*

Circle the letter of the best answer for each question.

5. What did Chuck Yeager do in 1947?

   a. traveled faster than sound

   b. slowed the speed of sound

   c. explained the properties of sound

   d. flew across the Atlantic Ocean

PITCH AND FREQUENCY

6. Which of these things is NOT related to pitch?

   a. frequency of sound waves

   b. number of Hertz

   c. number of waves per second

   d. distance to the sound's source

7. What is a measure of how high or how low a sound seems to be?

   a. pitch

   b. frequency

   c. speed

   d. medium

Frequency and Hearing

8. What is true about the sound from a dog whistle?

   a. has a low frequency

   b. has a low pitch

   c. cannot be heard by dogs

   d. is an ultrasonic sound

The Doppler Effect

9. What causes a car horn to change pitch as the car passes you?

   a. frequency   **c.** rarefaction

   b. Doppler effect   **d.** compression

Copyright © by Holt, Rinehart and Winston. All rights reserved.

Directed Reading B *continued*

Circle the letter of the best answer for each question.

10. When a sound wave moves in the same direction as the hearer, what gets closer together?

   a. pitch and frequency

   b. compressions and rarefactions

   c. car and listener

   d. Doppler effect and sound waves

11. How does the pitch of a moving car horn sound to the person in front of it?

   a. higher than to the driver

   b. lower than to the driver

   c. the same as to the driver

   d. higher then lower in pitch

12. How does the pitch of a moving car horn sound to the person behind it?

   a. higher than to the driver

   b. lower than to the driver

   c. the same as to the driver

   d. higher then lower in pitch

LOUDNESS AND AMPLITUDE

13. What word describes how well a sound can be heard?

   a. decibel

   b. loudness

   c. amplitude

   d. frequency

Copyright © by Holt, Rinehart and Winston. All rights reserved.

| Directed Reading B *continued*

Energy and Vibration
Circle the letter of the best answer for each question.

14. What happens if you strike a drum harder?

    a. You give it more energy.

    b. The drums vibrations are smaller.

    c. Air particles vibrate less.

    d. The drums makes a softer sound.

Increasing Amplitude

15. What is the largest distance particles in a wave vibrate from their resting place?

    a. decibel

    b. loudness

    c. amplitude

    d. frequency

Measuring Loudness

16. What is the unit for loudness or softness?

    a. decibel

    b. loudness

    c. frequency

    d. amplitude

Copyright © by Holt, Rinehart and Winston. All rights reserved.

Directed Reading B *continued*

"SEEING" AMPLITUDE AND FREQUENCY

Use the graphs below to answer questions 17 and 18. For each question, <u>circle the letter</u> before the words that best answer the question.

A 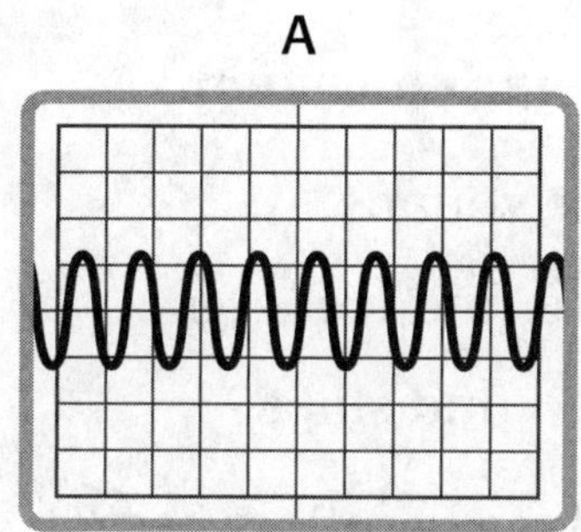 B 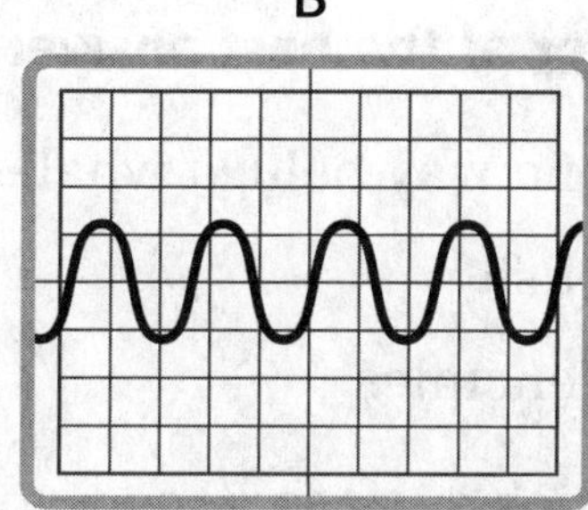

17. Look at the graphs. What is true about sound B?

    a. It has a lower pitch.

    b. It is louder.

    c. It has a larger amplitude.

    d. It has a higher pitch.

From Sound to Electrical Signal

18. Look at the graphs. What do high points of the lines represent?

    a. rarefactions

    b. compressions

    c. sound waves

    d. decibels

<u>Circle the letter</u> of the best answer for each question.

19. What is an oscilloscope used for?

    a. measures loudness

    b. changes pitch

    c. measures amplitude

    d. graphs sound waves

Copyright © by Holt, Rinehart and Winston. All rights reserved.

Directed Reading B

Section: Interactions of Sound Waves
REFLECTION OF SOUND WAVES

Circle the letter of the best answer for each question.

1. What is one way beluga whales use sounds?

   a. to find fish

   b. to find enemies

   c. to find icebergs

   d. to find ships

2. Off of which surface does a sound wave reflect best?

   a. soft

   b. shiny

   c. hard and smooth

   d. irregularly shaped

Read the words in the box. Read the sentences. Fill in each blank with the word or phrase that best completes the sentence.

Doppler effect	sonar	echo
reflection	echolocation	

3. The bouncing back of a wave after it strikes a barrier is called a(n) _____________________.

4. A reflected sound wave is a(n) _________________________.

Echolocation

5. The use of reflected sounds by animals to find objects is _____________________.

6. Bats using echoes to tell if insects are flying toward them are using the _____________________.

Echolocation Technology

7. Electronic echolocation is called _________________________.

Copyright © by Holt, Rinehart and Winston. All rights reserved.

Directed Reading B *continued*

Ultrasonography

Circle the letter of the best answer for each question.

8. What do doctors use to "see" inside a patient's body?

   a. echolocation

   b. ultrasonography

   c. X rays

   d. interference

INTERFERENCE OF SOUND WAVES

Read the words in the box. Read the sentences. Fill in each blank with the word or phrase that best completes the sentence.

sonic boom	constructive
destructive	interference

9. When two or more waves overlap, _______________________________

occurs.

10. In _______________________ interference, two sound waves

overlap to make a softer sound.

11. In _______________________ interference, two sound waves

join to make a louder sound.

12. When an airplane travels faster than sound, a(n)

_______________________ occurs.

Copyright © by Holt, Rinehart and Winston. All rights reserved.

❙ Directed Reading B *continued*

Interference and the Sound Barrier

Use the diagram below to answer questions 13–15. For each question, circle the letter before the words that best answer the question.

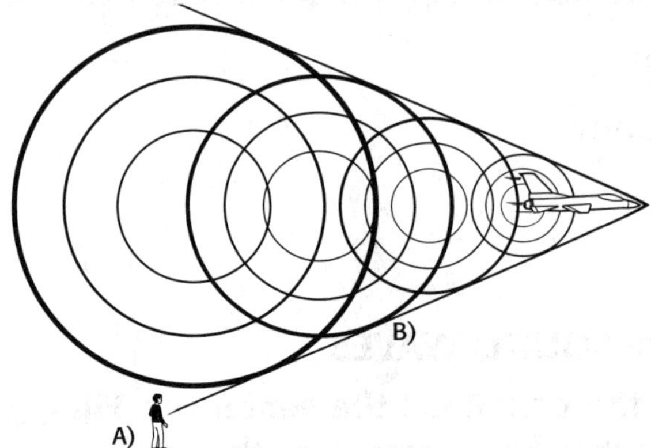

13. Look at the diagram. When does the person at point A hear the sonic boom?

   a. when the jet breaks the sound barrier

   b. when the shock waves reach the person

   c. when the jet travels faster than sound

   d. when the sonic boom occurs

14. Look at the diagram. What happens at point B?

   a. deconstructive interference

   b. shock wave is produced

   c. sonic boom is produced

   d. supersonic speeds

15. Look at the diagram. What do the circles show?

   a. sonic booms

   b. shock waves

   c. sound waves

   d. supersonic speeds

Copyright © by Holt, Rinehart and Winston. All rights reserved.

Directed Reading B *continued*

Interference and Standing Waves

Circle the letter of the best answer for each question.

16. What kind of wave looks like a wave that is standing still?

 a. interference wave

 b. standing wave

 c. resonant wave

 d. fundamental wave

RESONANCE

17. What frequency must a guitar string have if a tuning fork can make it vibrate?

 a. one of the resonant frequencies

 b. all of the resonant frequencies

 c. none of the resonant frequencies

 d. frequency doesn't matter

18. What is it called when the vibration of one object causes another to vibrate?

 a. frequency

 b. standing wave

 c. Doppler effect

 d. resonance

Resonance in Musical Instruments

19. Which of these helps a guitar use resonance to make sounds?

 a. compression waves

 b. blowing into a mouthpiece

 c. a hollow body

 d. Doppler effect

Copyright © by Holt, Rinehart and Winston. All rights reserved.

Skills Worksheet

Directed Reading B

Section: Sound Quality
Circle the letter of the best answer for each question.

1. What is the difference between music and sound?

   a. loudness

   b. pitch

   c. amplitude

   d. sound quality

WHAT IS SOUND QUALITY?

2. Why do the same notes sound different on different instruments?

   a. They have different volumes.

   b. Each has one pitch.

   c. They have the same overtones.

   d. They have different sound qualities.

3. What is the result of several pitches mixing through interference?

   a. constructive interference

   b. sound quality

   c. overtones

   d. fundamental frequency

SOUND QUALITY OF INSTRUMENTS

4. What causes different sound qualities in different instruments?

   a. differences in structure

   b. differences in size

   c. differences in frequencies

   d. differences in pitch

Copyright © by Holt, Rinehart and Winston. All rights reserved.

Directed Reading B *continued*

String Instruments

<u>Circle the letter</u> **of the best answer for each question.**

5. What affects the pitch of a string instrument?

  a. length of string

  b. length of bow

  c. amplifier

  d. resonating in body

6. What makes a higher frequency in a string instrument?

  a. longer string

  b. shorter string

  c. thicker string

  d. longer bow

Wind Instruments

7. What happens at the end of its air column in a wind instrument?

  a. standing waves

  b. vibrations

  c. opening finger holes

  d. woodwinds

8. Which is a brass instrument?

  a. clarinet

  b. oboe

  c. trombone

  d. recorder

Copyright © by Holt, Rinehart and Winston. All rights reserved.

Directed Reading B *continued*

Percussion Instruments

Circle the letter of the best answer for each question.

9. What is needed to get a lower sound from a percussion instrument?

a. smaller instrument

b. larger instrument

c. cymbals

d. drum

MUSIC OR NOISE?

10. What is a sound that is made up of a random mix of frequencies?

a. overtone

b. resonance

c. music

d. noise

11. Which would produce a sound wave with a repeating pattern?

a. slamming a door

b. French horn

c. keys falling to the floor

d. truck engine

12. What will you see on an oscilloscope graph of a sharp clap?

a. repeating pattern

b. straight line

c. random mix of frequencies

d. overtones

Copyright © by Holt, Rinehart and Winston. All rights reserved.

Skills Worksheet

Vocabulary and Section Summary

What Is Sound?

VOCABULARY

In your own words, write a definition of the following terms in the space provided.

1. sound wave

____

____

2. medium

____

____

SECTION SUMMARY

Read the following section summary.

- All sounds are generated by vibrations.

- Sounds travel as longitudinal waves consisting of compressions and rarefactions.

- Sound waves travel in all directions away from their source.

- Sound waves require a medium through which to travel. Sound cannot travel in a vacuum.

- Your ears convert sound into electrical impulses that are sent to your brain.

- Exposure to loud sounds can cause hearing damage.

- Using earplugs and lowering the volume of sounds can prevent hearing damage.

Copyright © by Holt, Rinehart and Winston. All rights reserved.

Name _______________________________ Class _____________ Date ___________

Vocabulary and Section Summary

Properties of Sound

VOCABULARY

In your own words, write a definition of the following terms in the space provided.

1. pitch

____

____

2. Doppler effect

____

____

3. loudness

____

____

4. decibel

____

____

SECTION SUMMARY

Read the following section summary.

- The speed of sound depends on the medium and the temperature.

- The pitch of a sound becomes higher as the frequency of the sound wave becomes higher. Frequency is expressed in units of Hertz (Hz), which is equivalent to waves per second.

- The Doppler effect is the apparent change in frequency of a sound caused by the motion of either the listener or the source of the sound.

- Loudness increases with the amplitude of the sound. Loudness is expressed in decibels.

- The amplitude and frequency of a sound can be measured electronically by an oscilloscope.

Copyright © by Holt, Rinehart and Winston. All rights reserved.

Skills Worksheet

Vocabulary and Section Summary

Interactions of Sound Waves

VOCABULARY

In your own words, write a definition of the following terms in the space provided.

1. echo

____

____

2. echolocation

____

____

3. interference

____

____

4. sonic boom

____

____

5. standing wave

____

____

6. resonance

____

____

Copyright © by Holt, Rinehart and Winston. All rights reserved.

Vocabulary and Section Summary *continued*

SECTION SUMMARY

Read the following section summary.

- Echoes are reflected sound waves.
- Some animals can use echolocation to find food or to navigate around objects.
- People use echolocation technology in many underwater applications.
- Ultrasonography uses sound reflection for medical applications.
- Sound barriers and shock waves are created by interference.
- Standing waves form at an object's resonant frequencies.
- Resonance happens when a vibrating object causes a second object to vibrate at one of its resonant frequencies.

Copyright © by Holt, Rinehart and Winston. All rights reserved.

Skills Worksheet)

Vocabulary and Section Summary

Sound Quality

VOCABULARY

In your own words, write a definition of the following terms in the space provided.

1. sound quality

____

____

2. noise

____

____

SECTION SUMMARY

Read the following section summary.

- Different instruments have different sound qualities.
- Sound quality results from the blending through interference of the fundamental and several overtones.
- The three families of instruments are string instruments, wind instruments, and percussion.
- Noise is a sound consisting of a random mix of frequencies.

Copyright © by Holt, Rinehart and Winston. All rights reserved.

Skills Worksheet

Section Review

What Is Sound?

USING KEY TERMS

1. Use the following terms in the same sentence: *sound wave* and *medium*.

____

____

UNDERSTANDING KEY IDEAS

______ **2.** Sound travels as
    a. transverse waves.
    b. longitudinal waves.
    c. shock waves.
    d. airwaves.

______ **3.** Which part of the ear increases the size of the vibrations of sound waves entering the ear?
    a. outer ear
    b. ear canal
    c. middle ear
    d. inner ear

4. Name two ways of protecting your hearing.

____

____

CRITICAL THINKING

5. Analyzing Processes Explain why a person at a rock concert will not feel gusts of wind coming out of the speakers.

____

____

____

6. Analyzing Ideas If a meteorite crashed on the moon, would you be able to hear it on Earth? Why, or why not?

____

____

____

Copyright © by Holt, Rinehart and Winston. All rights reserved.

Section Review *continued*

7. Identifying Relationships Recall the breaking dishes mentioned at the beginning of this section. Why was the sound that they made so loud?

____

____

INTERPRETING GRAPHICS

The diagram below shows a diagram of a wave. Use the diagram to answer the questions that follow.

8. What kind of wave is this?

____

____

9. Label the compressions and rarefactions on the diagram.

10. How do vibrations make these kinds of waves?

____

____

Copyright © by Holt, Rinehart and Winston. All rights reserved.

Skills Worksheet

Section Review

Properties of Sound

USING KEY TERMS

1. In your own words, write a definition for the term *pitch*.

____

2. Use the following terms in the same sentence: *loudness* and *decibel*.

____

____

UNDERSTANDING KEY IDEAS

______ **3.** At the same temperature, in which medium does sound travel fastest?
  a. air
  b. liquid
  c. solid
  d. It travels at the same speed through all media.

4. In general, how does the temperature of a medium affect the speed of sound through that medium?

____

____

5. What property of waves affects the pitch of a sound?

____

____

6. How does an oscilloscope allow sound waves to be "seen"?

____

____

Copyright © by Holt, Rinehart and Winston. All rights reserved.

Section Review *continued*

MATH SKILLS

7. You see a distant flash of lightning, and then you hear a thunderclap 2 s later. The sound of the thunder moves at 343 m/s. How far away was the lightning? Show your work below.

8. In water that is near 0°C, a submarine sends out a sonar signal (a sound wave). It travels 1500 m/s and reaches an underwater mountain in 4 s. How far away is the mountain? Show your work below.

CRITICAL THINKING

9. Analyzing Processes Will a listener notice the Doppler effect if both the listener and the source of the sound are traveling toward each other? Explain your answer.

____

____

____

____

10. Predicting Consequences A drum is struck gently, then is struck harder. What will be the difference in the amplitude of the sounds made? What will be the difference in the frequency of the sounds made?

____

____

____

____

Copyright © by Holt, Rinehart and Winston. All rights reserved.

Skills Worksheet)

Section Review

Interactions of Sound Waves

USING KEY TERMS

1. Use the following terms in the same sentence: *echo* and *echolocation*.

____

____

Complete each of the following sentences by choosing the correct term from the word bank.

interference	standing wave
sonic boom	resonance

2. When you pluck a string on a musical instrument, a(n)

___________________________ forms.

3. When a vibrating object causes a nearby object to vibrate,

___________________________ results.

UNDERSTANDING KEY IDEAS

_______ **4.** What causes an echo?
   a. reflection
   b. resonance
   c. constructive interference
   d. destructive interference

5. Describe a place in which you would expect to hear echoes.

____

____

6. How do bats use echoes to find insects to eat?

____

____

7. Give one example each of constructive and destructive interference of sound waves.

____

____

Copyright © by Holt, Rinehart and Winston. All rights reserved.

Section Review *continued*

MATH SKILLS

8. Sound travels through air at 343 m/s at 20°C. A bat emits an ultrasonic squeak and hears the echo 0.05 s later. How far away was the object that reflected it? (Hint: Remember that the sound must travel to the object and back to the bat.) Show your work below.

CRITICAL THINKING

9. Applying Concepts Your friend is playing a song on a piano. Whenever your friend hits a certain key, the lamp on top of the piano rattles. Explain why this happens.

____

____

____

____

10. Making Comparisons Compare sonar and ultrasonography in locating objects.

____

____

____

____

Copyright © by Holt, Rinehart and Winston. All rights reserved.

Skills Worksheet

Section Review

Sound Quality
USING KEY TERMS

1. Use each of the following terms in a separate sentence: *sound quality* and *noise*.

____

____

UNDERSTANDING KEY IDEAS

______ **2.** What interaction of sound waves determines sound quality?
- **a.** reflection
- **b.** diffraction
- **c.** pitch
- **d.** interference

3. Why do different instruments have different sound qualities?

____

____

CRITICAL THINKING

4. Making Comparisons What do string instruments and wind instruments have in common in how they produce sound?

____

____

____

____

5. Identifying Bias Someone says that the music you are listening to is "just noise." Does the person mean that the music is a random mix of frequencies? Explain.

____

____

____

Copyright © by Holt, Rinehart and Winston. All rights reserved.

Section Review *continued*

INTERPRETING GRAPHICS

6. Look at the oscilloscope screen below. Do you think the sound represented by the wave on the screen is noise or music? Explain your answer.

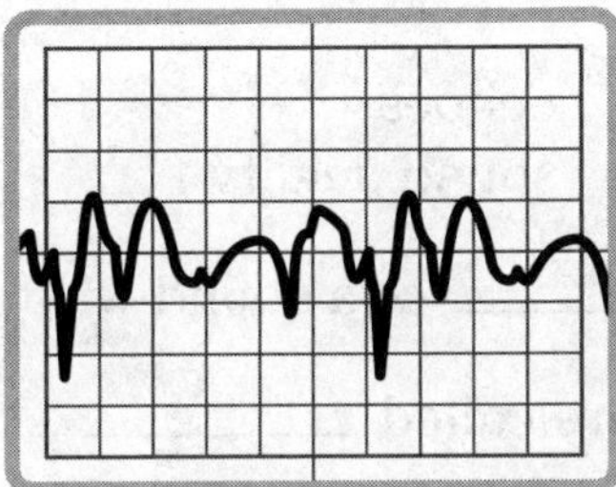

____

____

____

____

____

Copyright © by Holt, Rinehart and Winston. All rights reserved.

Skills Worksheet)

Chapter Review

USING KEY TERMS

Complete each of the following sentences by choosing the correct term from the word bank.

loudness   echoes   pitch

noise   sound quality

1. The _____________________ of a sound wave depends on its amplitude.

2. Reflected sound waves are called _____________________.

3. Two different instruments playing the same note sound different because

of _____________________.

UNDERSTANDING KEY IDEAS

Multiple Choice

______ **4.** If a fire engine is traveling toward you, the Doppler effect will cause
the siren to sound
    a. higher.   **c.** louder.
    b. lower.   **d.** softer.

______ **5.** Sound travels fastest through
    a. a vacuum.   **c.** air.
    b. sea water.   **d.** glass.

______ **6.** If two sound waves interfere constructively, you will hear
    a. a high-pitched sound.
    b. a softer sound.
    c. a louder sound.
    d. no change in sound.

______ **7.** You will hear a sonic boom when
    a. an object breaks the sound barrier.
    b. an object travels at supersonic speeds.
    c. a shock wave reaches your ears.
    d. the speed of sound is 290 m/s.

______ **8.** Resonance can happen when an object vibrates at another object's
    a. resonant frequency.
    b. fundamental frequency.
    c. second overtone frequency.
    d. All of the above

Copyright © by Holt, Rinehart and Winston. All rights reserved.

Chapter Review *continued*

______ **9.** A technological device that can be used to see sound waves is a(n)
  a. sonar. **c.** ultrasound.
  b. oscilloscope. **d.** amplifier.

Short Answer

10. Describe how the Doppler effect helps a beluga whale determine whether a fish is moving away from it or toward it.

____

____

____

11. How do vibrations cause sound waves?

____

____

____

12. Briefly describe what happens in the different parts of the ear.

____

____

____

MATH SKILLS

13. A submarine that is not moving sends out a sonar sound wave traveling 1,500 m/s, which reflects off a boat back to the submarine. The sonar crew detects the reflected wave 6 s after it was sent out. How far away is the boat from the submarine? Show your work below.

Copyright © by Holt, Rinehart and Winston. All rights reserved.

Chapter Review *continued*

CRITICAL THINKING

14. Concept Mapping Use the following terms to create a concept map: *sound waves, pitch, loudness, decibels, frequency, amplitude, oscilloscope, hertz,* and *interference.*

Copyright © by Holt, Rinehart and Winston. All rights reserved.

| Chapter Review *continued*

---

15. Analyzing Processes An *anechoic chamber* is a room where there is almost no reflection of sound waves. Anechoic chambers are often used to test sound equipment, such as stereos. The walls of such chambers are usually covered with foam triangles. Explain why this design eliminates echoes in the room.

____

____

____

16. Applying Concepts Would the pilot of an airplane breaking the sound barrier hear a sonic boom? Explain why or why not.

____

____

____

17. Forming Hypotheses After working in a factory for a month, a man you know complains about a ringing in his ears. What might be wrong with him? What do you think may have caused his problem? What can you suggest to him to prevent further hearing loss?

____

____

____

____

Copyright © by Holt, Rinehart and Winston. All rights reserved.

INTERPRETING GRAPHICS

Use the oscilloscope screens below to answer the questions that follow:

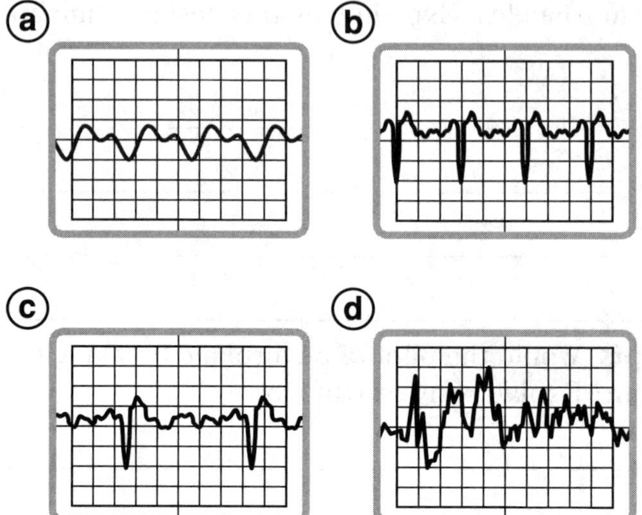

_______**18.** Which sound is noise?

_______**19.** Which represents the softest sound?

_______**20.** Which represents the sound with the lowest pitch?

_______**21.** Which two sounds were produced by the same instrument?

Copyright © by Holt, Rinehart and Winston. All rights reserved.

Name _________________________________ Class _______________ Date ____________

Reinforcement

Doppler Dan's Dump Truck

Complete this worksheet after you finish reading the section "Properties of Sound."

Doppler Dan the Garbage Man is moving a truckload of glass from one end of the recycling plant to the other. Elinor has just helped him load up all of the broken bottles at the front of the plant on the east side of the lot. As Dan drives away, he honks his horn in thanks to Elinor. He speeds off in a hurry, because his buddy Otis is waiting impatiently on the west side to help him unload the glass from the dump truck.

"Howdy, Otis," says Dan, as he drives up.

"Hey," grumbles Otis, chewing on his pen. "Your horn sounds funny."

"Sounds fine to me," says Dan, as cheerfully as possible. He thinks Otis is just making trouble, as he is not a morning person. Still it seems like a strange thing to say. Why would the horn sound different to Otis than it did to him?

At the end of the day, Dan was still wondering about Otis's mysterious comment. He decided to ask Elinor about it.

Elinor reminds Dan that he honked the horn as he drove away from her. Then she draws him the diagram below. Points 0–3 represent Dan's positions as he drove from east to west. The compressions of the sound waves made by the honking horn are shown as circles A–D. A is the compression that came from the horn when Dan was at Point 0, B is from Point 1, C is from Point 2, and D is from Point 3.

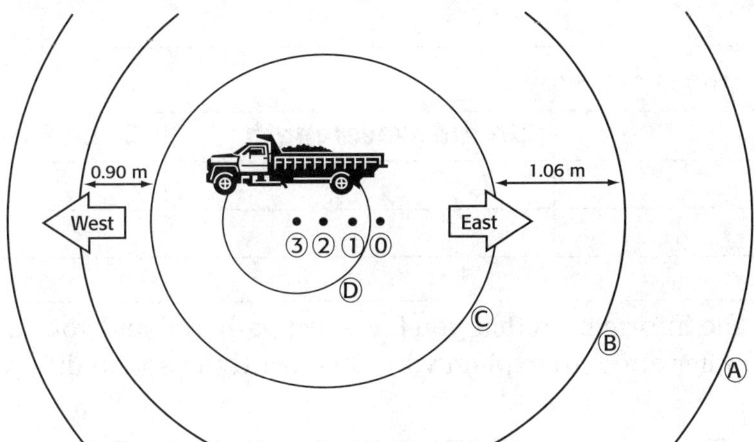

Next Elinor tells Dan that by studying the diagram and doing some minor calculations, he could find out the answer. On the next page, follow the steps Dan used to find out why the horn sounded different to Otis. The formulas below will help you.

Formulas

For the speed of a wave: wave speed = wavelength × frequency

For wavelength: wavelength = wave speed ÷ frequency

For frequency: frequency = wave speed ÷ wavelength

Copyright © by Holt, Rinehart and Winston. All rights reserved.

Reinforcement *continued*

1. Use your textbook to find the speed of sound in air at 20°C.

wave speed = ________________________.

2. Doppler Dan bought his horn from Honk, Inc. They guaranteed that the horn will honk at a frequency of 350 Hz. Use the equation on the previous page to calculate the wavelength of sound made by Dan's horn and show your work here.

____

____

3. Find the wavelength of the sound by measuring the distance from one compression to the next. From where Otis is standing, what is the wavelength of the sound?

____

4. The frequency of sound that you hear is the speed of the sound divided by the wavelength. What frequency did Otis hear?

____

5. What is the wavelength of the sound on the side of the dump truck where Elinor is standing?

____

6. What frequency did Elinor hear?

____

7. Complete the chart below.

Listener	Sound wavelength	Sound frequency
Dan		
Otis		
Elinor		

8. Now use the information that you have just gathered and your understanding of the Doppler effect to explain why Otis heard the sound differently than Dan.

____

____

____

Copyright © by Holt, Rinehart and Winston. All rights reserved.

Skills Worksheet

Critical Thinking

The Noise Police

While patrolling your beat in the pulsing town of Harmony, you receive the following police dispatch:

Squad car 27, please investigate the following disturbances:

- A report of loud noise coming from a downtown dog show was filed by Ms. L. V. Katz. She claims to be disturbed by sounds registering frequencies of over 20,000 Hz.

- Community members living near the city coliseum are complaining of jazz music that is in excess of 120 decibels.

- A call was received from Mr. Sy Lentz on Oak Street. His neighbor, Mr. Billy Bob Mozart, is playing loud classical music, probably a tuba concerto. He is playing off-key. All the notes are too low.

USEFUL TERMS

decibel meter a meter or gauge used to measure the decibel levels of sound waves

UNDERSTANDING CONCEPTS

1. Is the complaint about the dog-show noise valid? Explain.

____

____

____

____

2. The music in the city coliseum is loud, but it does not register too high on your decibel meter. It is hard to hear music in certain parts of the building. Explain what might cause this.

____

____

____

____

____

Copyright © by Holt, Rinehart and Winston. All rights reserved.

▌Critical Thinking *continued*

COMPREHENDING IDEAS

3. How could the coliseum's walls be designed to contain the sound waves from the concert so that the neighbors are not disturbed?

____

____

____

____

____

4. Mr. Mozart plays classical music on the tuba, but he is also going deaf. What can he do in order to get his instrument to play more on key? Explain why this will help.

____

____

____

____

____

5. On the way home from your patrol, you pass a parked car whose driver is honking the horn. The sound of the horn changes pitch as you drive by. Explain why this happens.

____

____

____

____

____

Copyright © by Holt, Rinehart and Winston. All rights reserved.

Name _________________________________ Class ______________ Date __________

Assessment

Section Quiz

Section: What Is Sound?

Write the letter of the correct answer in the space provided.

_______ **1.** Sound is created by
   a. the complete back-and-forth motion of objects.
   b. air particles slowing down.
   c. longitudinal waves.
   d. a substance through which sound can move.

_______ **2.** A substance through which a wave can travel is a
   a. longitudinal wave.   **c.** medium.
   b. vibration.   **d.** rarefaction.

_______ **3.** Which of the following is NOT a medium?
   a. a glass window   **c.** a metal fork
   b. a vacuum   **d.** the ocean

_______ **4.** One thing you can do to protect your hearing is to
   a. sit in the back of the room during a rock concert.
   b. use earphones when listening to the radio.
   c. eat a nutritious and balanced diet.
   d. sleep in a darkened room.

Use the figure below to answer questions 5 through 7. Write the letter of the correct answer in the space provided.

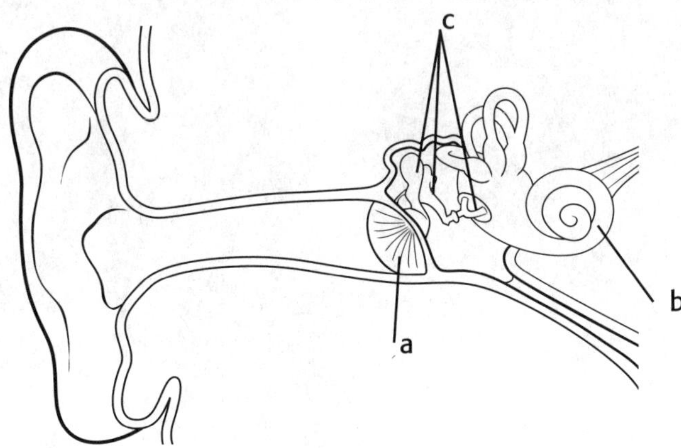

_______ **5.** Which part of the ear increases the size of the vibrations?

_______ **6.** Which part of the ear do sound waves have to pass through in order to get from the outer ear to the middle ear?

_______ **7.** Which part of the ear contains a liquid and tiny hairs?

Copyright © by Holt, Rinehart and Winston. All rights reserved.

Section Quiz

Section: Properties of Sound

Match the correct definition with the correct term. Write the letter in the space provided.

_______ **1.** speed of sound varies from one to another

_______ **2.** how high or low a sound seems to be

_______ **3.** units for expressing frequency

_______ **4.** Sounds with 120 of these units can be painful.

_______ **5.** causes a sound in front of a moving sound source to seem to have a higher pitch and frequency

_______ **6.** sounds that have a frequency too high for people to hear

_______ **7.** a measure of how well a sound can be heard

_______ **8.** used to graph representations of sound wave

_______ **9.** represented by the troughs on a graph from an oscilloscope

_______ **10.** When it is larger, the sound is louder.

a. pitch

b. oscilloscope

c. Hertz

d. medium

e. Doppler effect

f. rarefactions

g. decibels

h. amplitude

i. loudness

j. ultrasonic

Copyright © by Holt, Rinehart and Winston. All rights reserved.

Assessment

Section Quiz

Section: Interactions of Sound Waves

Match the correct definition with the correct term. Write the letter in the space provided.

_______ **1.** technology that uses echoes to locate objects

_______ **2.** a medical procedure used to check the development of an unborn baby in a mother's body

_______ **3.** explosive sound heard when shock waves arrive at a person's ears

_______ **4.** process in which a dolphin uses reflected waves to determine how far away objects are

_______ **5.** interference used by a band when several instruments play the same note

_______ **6.** a reflected sound wave

_______ **7.** formed at a fundamental frequency or an overtone

_______ **8.** interference that may cause people not to hear sounds in an auditorium

_______ **9.** when two or more waves combine to form a single wave

_______ **10.** occurs when a vibrating tuning fork causes a rubber band to vibrate

a. echo

b. echolocation

c. interference

d. sonic boom

e. standing wave

f. resonance

g. destructive

h. constructive

i. sonar

j. ultrasonography

Copyright © by Holt, Rinehart and Winston. All rights reserved.

Assessment

Section Quiz

Section: Sound Quality

Write the letter of the correct answer in the space provided.

_______ **1.** Different instruments produce their own unique sound qualities because
    a. each one is played by a musician with a different amount of experience.
    b. each has several different pitches that mix together through resonance.
    c. each has several different pitches that mix together through interference.
    d. some produce fundamental frequencies and some produce overtones.

_______ **2.** What can a violinist do if one string is producing a sound that is too low?
    a. lengthen the string
    b. shorten the string
    c. attach the violin to an amplifier
    d. use a longer bow

_______ **3.** Which of the following sequences is correct?
    a. bridge vibrates; string vibrates; body of viola vibrates; resonance occurs
    b. body of viola vibrates; bridge vibrates; string vibrates; resonance occurs
    c. resonance occurs; bridge vibrates; string vibrates; body of viola vibrates
    d. string vibrates; bridge vibrates; body of viola vibrates; resonance occurs

_______ **4.** Which of the following will produce a noise?
    a. a car motor
    b. a guitar
    c. a drum
    d. a bass saxophone

_______ **5.** What produces a noise?
    a. a repeating pattern of frequencies
    b. a repeating pattern of amplitudes
    c. a random mix of volumes
    d. a random mix of frequencies

Copyright © by Holt, Rinehart and Winston. All rights reserved.

Chapter Test A

The Nature of Sound

MULTIPLE CHOICE

Write the letter of the correct answer in the space provided.

_______ **1.** The blending of pitches through interference produces an instrument's
   a. sound quality.
   b. amplitude.
   c. echoes.
   d. resonance.

_______ **2.** The amplitude of a sound's waves determines the sound's
   a. pitch.
   b. loudness.
   c. resonance.
   d. sound quality.

_______ **3.** Sounds with frequencies higher than 20,000 Hz
   a. result from standing waves.
   b. create destructive interference.
   c. are considered to be noise.
   d. are ultrasonic sounds.

_______ **4.** The motion of either the listener or the source of a sound causes
   a. resonance.
   b. shock waves.
   c. the Doppler effect.
   d. echolocation.

_______ **5.** The frequency of a sound wave determines
   a. the pitch of the sound.
   b. the loudness of the sound.
   c. the sound quality.
   d. the type of interference.

_______ **6.** Which statement about sound is NOT true?
   a. Air particles travel with sound waves.
   b. Sound waves cannot travel through a vacuum.
   c. Sound waves exist even if no one hears them.
   d. Air particles vibrate along the path of a sound wave.

_______ **7.** An echo is most likely to result when sound hits a surface that is
   a. bumpy and soft.   **c.** smooth and hard.
   b. smooth and soft.   **d.** bumpy and hard.

Copyright © by Holt, Rinehart and Winston. All rights reserved.

Chapter Test A *continued*

_______ **8.** The medium through which sound waves travel affects the
    a. speed of the sound.
    b. the amplitude of the waves.
    c. the number of waves per second.
    d. the sound quality.

_______ **9.** A person experiences a sonic boom when
    a. a shock wave reaches the ears.
    b. an airplane breaks the sound barrier.
    c. overtones are created.
    d. sound waves overlap by constructive interference.

MATCHING

Match the description with the correct term. Write the letter in the space provided.

_______**10.** vibrates when struck

_______**11.** vibration causes standing waves inside its air column

_______**12.** the use of reflected sound waves to find food or other objects

_______**13.** occurs when two instruments play the same note

_______**14.** the sound produced by one object causes another object to vibrate

_______**15.** longitudinal wave caused by vibrations and carried through a medium

_______**16.** a pattern of vibration that looks like a wave is at rest

_______**17.** unit for measuring loudness

_______**18.** results from long-term exposure to loud sounds

_______**19.** frequencies two or more times the fundamental frequency

a. sound wave

b. echolocation

c. resonance

d. standing wave

e. decibel

f. overtones

g. interference

h. woodwind instrument

i. percussion instrument

j. tinnitus

Copyright © by Holt, Rinehart and Winston. All rights reserved.

Chapter Test A *continued*

MATCHING

Match the labels to the drawing. Write the letters in the spaces provided.

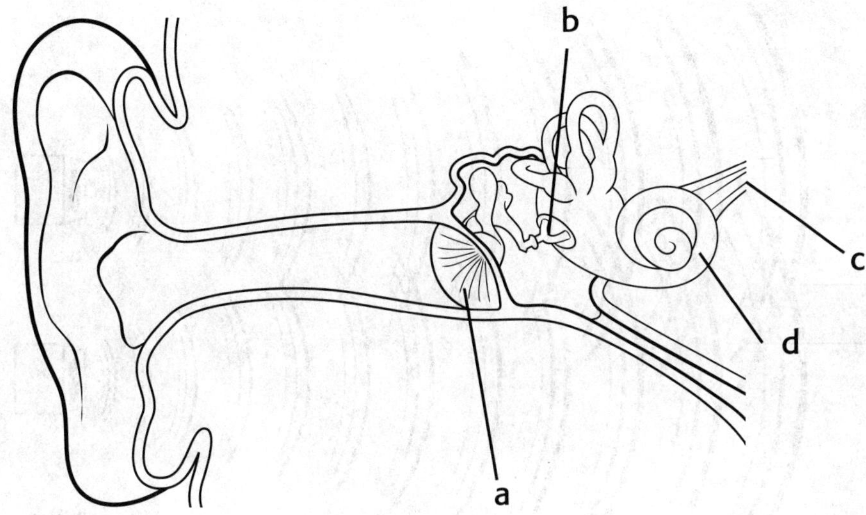

_______**20.** The vibrating stirrup causes the oval window to vibrate.

_______**21.** Electrical signals are sent to the brain due to stimulation of nerves by bending hair cells.

_______**22.** Sound waves cause the eardrum to vibrate.

_______**23.** Movement of liquid inside cochlea causes hair cells to bend.

Copyright © by Holt, Rinehart and Winston. All rights reserved.

MULTIPLE CHOICE

Use the figure below to answer questions 24 and 25. Write the letter of the correct answer in the space provided.

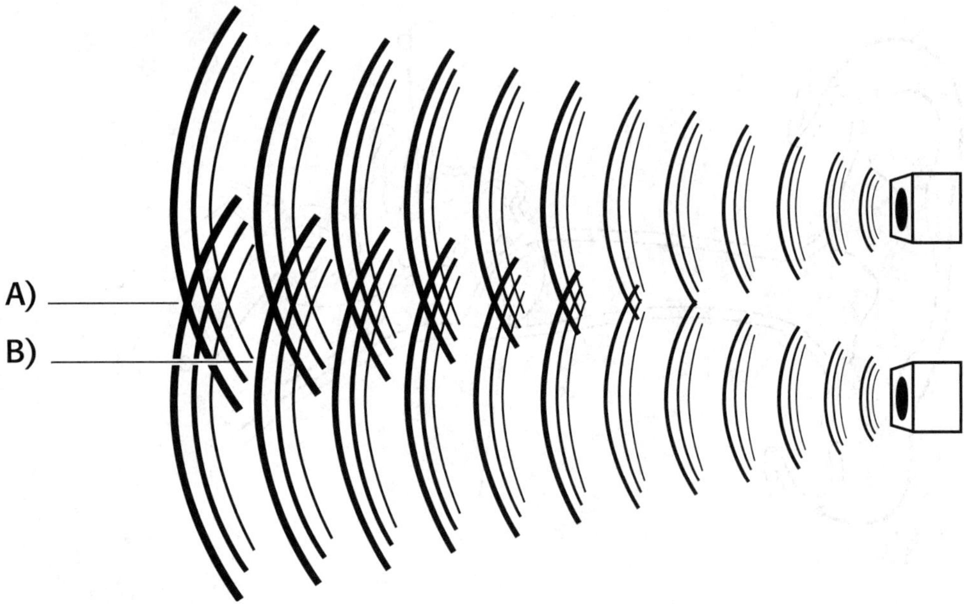

_______**24.** Look at the diagram. What happens at point A?

    a. Compressions of one wave overlap rarefactions of another to create a softer sound.

    b. Compressions of one wave overlap rarefactions of another to create a louder sound.

    c. Compressions of one wave overlap compressions of another to create a softer sound.

    d. Compressions of one wave overlap compressions of another to create a louder sound.

_______**25.** Look at the diagram. What happens at point B?

    a. The amplitude is decreased.

    b. The amplitude is increased.

    c. The frequency is increased.

    d. The frequency is decreased.

Copyright © by Holt, Rinehart and Winston. All rights reserved.

Chapter Test B

The Nature of Sound
USING KEY TERMS

Use the terms from the following list to complete the sentences below. Each term may be used only once. Some terms may not be used.

echolocation Doppler effect sound quality
pitch loudness ultrasonic
resonance

1. An instrument's ________________________ comes from the blending of pitches through interference.

2. The amplitude of a sound's waves determines its ________________________.

3. Sounds with frequencies higher than 20,000 Hz are

________________________.

4. The motion of either the listener or the source of a sound causes the

________________________.

5. The frequency of the sound wave determines its ________________________.

UNDERSTANDING KEY IDEAS

Write the letter of the correct answer in the space provided.

______ 6. Which statement about sound is true?
   a. Air particles travel with sound waves.
   b. Sound waves can travel through a vacuum.
   c. Sound waves exist only if someone hears them.
   d. Air particles vibrate along the path of a sound wave.

______ 7. Sound waves are best reflected off which surfaces?
   a. bumpy, soft
   b. smooth, soft
   c. smooth, hard
   d. bumpy, hard

______ 8. The speed of a sound depends on
   a. its source.
   b. the force of its compressions.
   c. the number of waves per second.
   d. the medium through which it travels.

Copyright © by Holt, Rinehart and Winston. All rights reserved.

_______ **9.** For a sound wave to produce an echo, it must
   a. diffract around a small barrier.
   b. reflect off the surface of an object.
   c. have an ultrasonic frequency.
   d. have a very long wavelength.

_______ **10.** A sonic boom is experienced when
   a. a shock wave reaches an observer.
   b. a moving object breaks the sound barrier.
   c. a jet engine's thrust is suddenly increased.
   d. sound waves overlap by destructive interference.

11. How is an oscilloscope used to "see" sound waves?

____

____

12. Explain the difference between constructive interference and destructive interference.

____

____

13. How are echoes used to locate underwater objects?

____

____

CRITICAL THINKING

14. Jeremy's parents do not like the music that he listens to. They call it noise and tell him to turn it down or turn it off. Jeremy wants to prove to his parents that it really is music. What could he do? Explain how his results might prove him or his parents correct.

____

____

____

15. Maria's little brother and sister have made a tin-can telephone, but they can't hear each other with it. What might be the problem? What tips should Maria give them so their toy will work better?

____

____

____

Copyright © by Holt, Rinehart and Winston. All rights reserved.

| Chapter Test B *continued*

---

16. For a science fair project, Terri wants to make a model to show how the ear detects sounds. What might her model look like, and how might it work?

____

____

____

CONCEPT MAPPING

17. Use the following terms to complete the concept map below:

middle portion	levers	ear canal
electrical signals	pinna	outer portion
vibrations	brain	

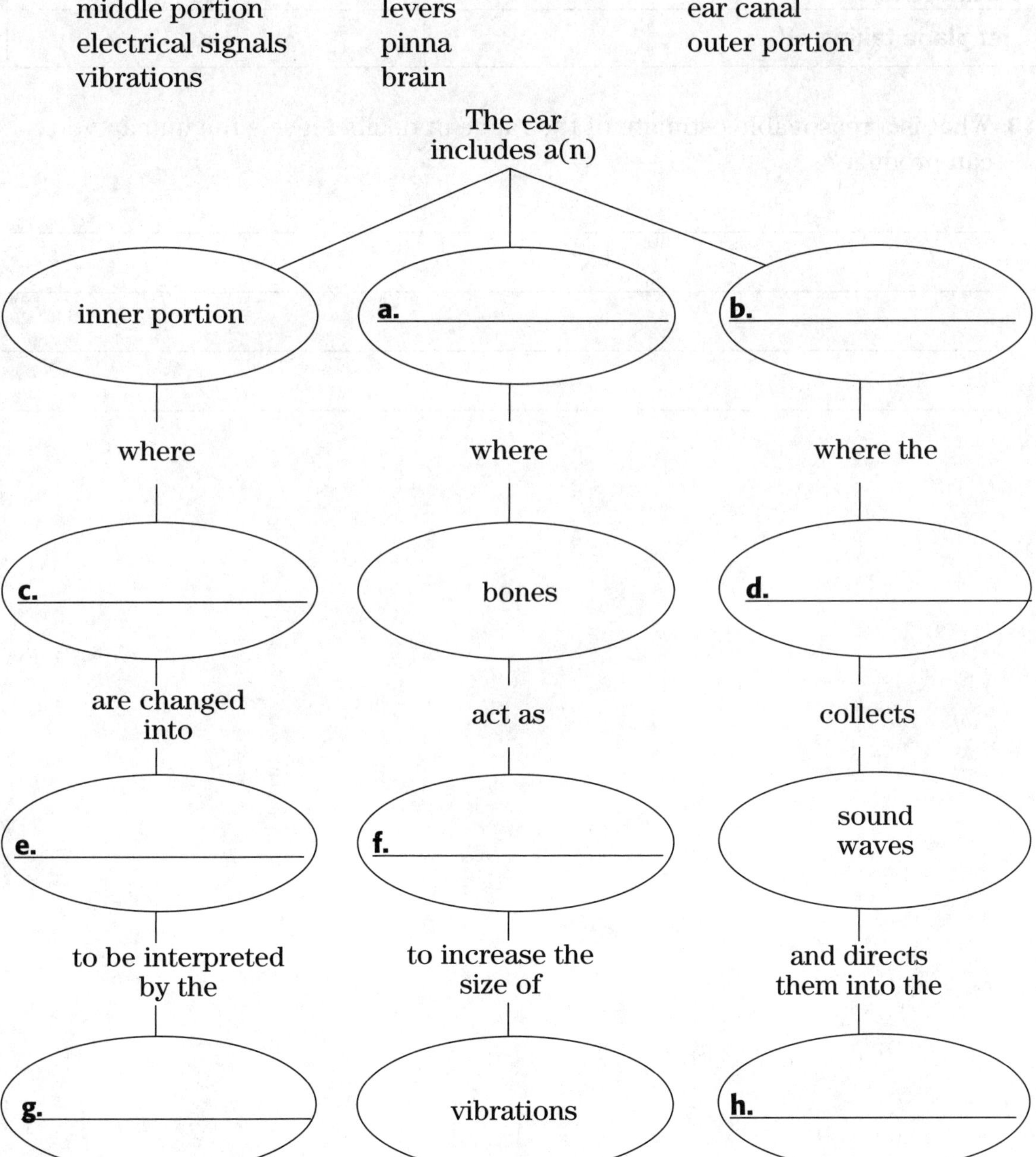

Copyright © by Holt, Rinehart and Winston. All rights reserved.

Name _____________________________________ Class _________________ Date _______________

INTERPRETING GRAPHICS

Use the chart below to answer question 18.

Sound	Decibel level
a soft whisper	20
leaves rustling	30
normal conversation	60
automobile accelerating	70
motorcycle engine	110
rock concert	120
jet plane taking off	140

18. What is a reasonable estimate of the range of decibel levels the human voice can produce?

____

____

____

____

Copyright © by Holt, Rinehart and Winston. All rights reserved.

Chapter Test C

The Nature of Sound

MULTIPLE CHOICE

<u>**Circle the letter**</u> **of the best answer for each question.**

1. What does the mixing of pitches through interference produce?

   a. sound quality

   b. amplitude

   c. echoes

   d. resonance

2. What does the amplitude of a sound's waves affect?

   a. pitch

   b. loudness

   c. resonance

   d. sound quality

3. What does the motion of the source of a sound cause?

   a. resonance

   b. shock waves

   c. the Doppler effect

   d. echolocation

4. What does the frequency of a sound wave affect?

   a. pitch

   b. loudness

   c. sound quality

   d. type of interference

5. Which statement about sound waves is true?

   a. Air travels with them.

   b. They travel through a vacuum.

   c. They exist only if heard.

   d. They can mix.

6. Which surface is the best reflector of sound?

   a. bumpy and soft

   b. smooth and soft

   c. smooth and hard

   d. bumpy and hard

7. What does the medium through which sound waves travel affect?

   a. speed of the sound

   b. amplitude of the waves

   c. number of waves per second

   d. sound quality

Copyright © by Holt, Rinehart and Winston. All rights reserved.

MATCHING

Read the description. Then, <u>draw a line</u> from the dot next to each description to the matching word.

8. A larger instrument has a lower sound. ●

9. Standing waves form inside its air column. ●

10. It is the use of reflected sound waves to find objects. ●

11. It occurs when two or more waves overlap. ●

12. The sound produced by one object causes another object to vibrate. ●

13. A part of the ear that contains a liquid. ●

a. cochlea

b. echolocation

c. resonance

d. interference

e. woodwind instrument

f. percussion instrument

Copyright © by Holt, Rinehart and Winston. All rights reserved.

Chapter Test C *continued*

FILL-IN-THE-BLANK

Read the words in the box. Read the sentences. <u>Fill in each blank</u> with the word or phrase that best completes the sentence.

pinna	oscilloscope	decibel
noise	standing wave	sonar

14. Sound is directed to the ear canal by the

_______________________.

15. The unit for measuring the loudness of sound is the

_______________________.

16. A sound with a random mixture of frequencies is

_______________________.

17. Electronic echolocation, or _______________________, is used

to find things underwater.

18. Part of a(n) _______________________ has a large amplitude

due to interference.

19. A graph of a sound can be made with a(n)

_______________________.

Copyright © by Holt, Rinehart and Winston. All rights reserved.

Chapter Test C *continued*

MULTIPLE CHOICE

Use the diagram below to answer questions 20–22. For each question, circle the letter of the best answer for each question.

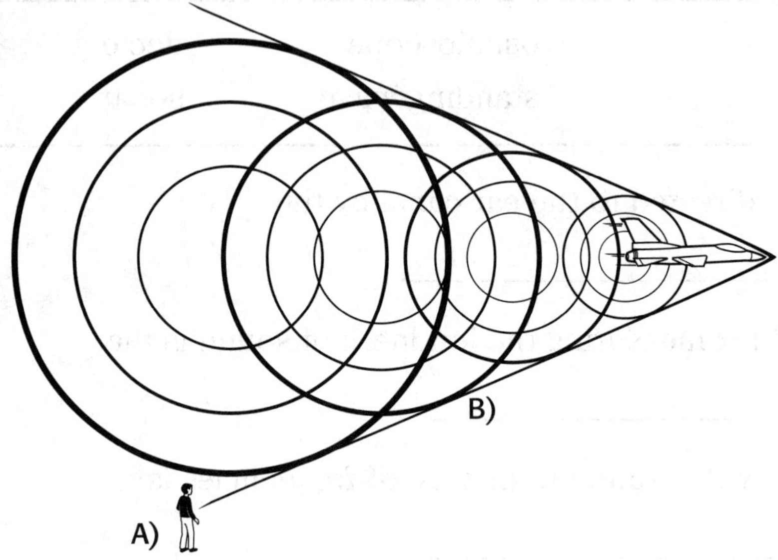

20. Look at the diagram. When does the person at point A hear the sonic boom?

   a. when the jet breaks the sound barrier

   b. when the shock waves reach the person

   c. when the jet travels faster than sound

   d. when the sonic boom occurs

21. Look at the diagram. What happens at point B?

   a. deconstructive interference

   b. shock wave is produced

   c. sonic boom is produced

   d. supersonic speeds

22. Look at the diagram. What do the circles show?

   a. sonic booms

   b. shock waves

   c. sound waves

   d. supersonic speeds

Copyright © by Holt, Rinehart and Winston. All rights reserved.

Performance-Based Assessment

OBJECTIVE

You will demonstrate differences in the way sound reflects off of various surfaces and use this information to investigate a real-life application.

KNOW THE SCORE!

As you work through the activity, keep in mind that you will be earning a grade for the following:

- how well you work with materials and equipment (30%)
- how well you state your observations (30%)
- how well you use your observations to answer analysis questions (40%)

MATERIALS AND EQUIPMENT

- table (at least 1.5 m long and 1 m wide)
- metric ruler
- 40 × 40 cm of poster board
- masking tape

- 2 cardboard tubes (each 50 cm long, 5 cm in diameter)
- clock that ticks
- 40 × 40 cm of terry cloth or bath towel
- 40 × 40 × 5 cm of foam rubber

Using Scientific Methods

ASK A QUESTION

How does sound respond when it hits different materials?

FORM A HYPOTHESIS

1. Your station has three different materials: poster board, terry cloth, and foam rubber. Which do you think will reflect sound the best? Which will absorb the most sound?

Material	What I hear
Poster board	
Terry cloth	
Foam rubber	

Copyright © by Holt, Rinehart and Winston. All rights reserved.

Performance-Based Assessment *continued*

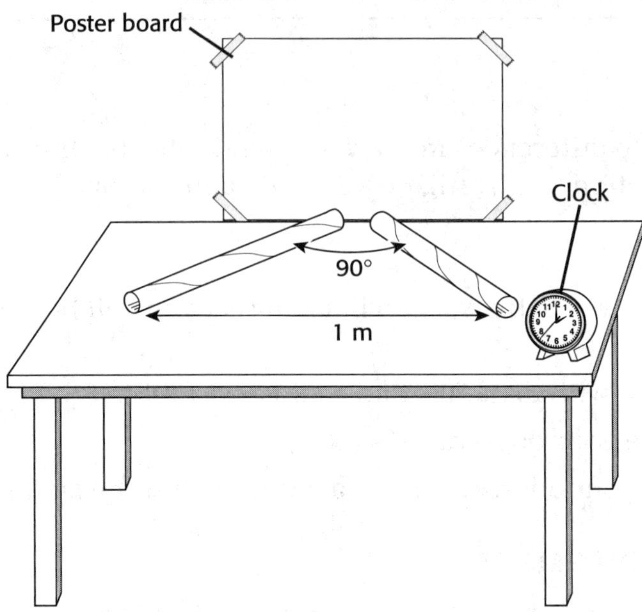

TEST THE HYPOTHESIS

2. Place the table 5 cm away from a wall.

3. Tape the poster board securely to the wall over the center of the table.

4. Place the cardboard tubes on the table so that one edge of each tube is approximately 5 cm from the poster board.

5. Arrange the cardboard tubes so that the ends that are closest to the poster board create a 90° angle to each other. The cardboard tubes should not touch each other.

6. The ends of the cardboard tubes that are farthest away from the poster board should be approximately 1 m apart.

7. Place the clock near the end of one of the cardboard tubes. You will be listening for the clock at the end of the other cardboard tube. The clock should be placed at the end of the cardboard tube that is farthest away from the poster board.

8. Check your setup by looking at the picture. Make any necessary changes.

9. Listen through the cardboard tube which does not have the clock in front of it. Make sure you hear it ticking. If you cannot hear the clock, adjust your setup.

10. Cover one ear, and put your other ear against the tube that is not next to the clock. Record the sound you hear in the table above.

11. Place the piece of terry cloth over the poster board. Repeat step 10, and record your observations.

12. Remove the fabric, and replace it with the piece of foam rubber. Repeat step 10 and record your observations.

Copyright © by Holt, Rinehart and Winston. All rights reserved.

Performance-Based Assessment *continued*

ANALYZE THE RESULTS

13. a. When was the sound the loudest?

____

b. When was the sound the softest?

____

14. What happens to sound waves that are not reflected?

____

DRAW CONCLUSIONS

15. Why did the sound change when different surfaces were used for reflection?

____

____

16. a. Concert halls are difficult to design because the designer must use both reflective and absorptive surfaces in order to achieve the best sound. What type of material would you use to reflect sound in a concert hall? Explain your answer.

____

____

b. What type of material would you use to absorb sound in a concert hall?

____

____

17. a. Why would you not want to use all soft materials inside a concert hall?

____

____

b. Why would you not want to use all hard materials inside a concert hall?

____

____

Copyright © by Holt, Rinehart and Winston. All rights reserved.

Standardized Test Preparation

READING

Read each of the passages below. Then, answer the questions that follow each passage.

Passage 1 Centuries ago, Marco Polo wrote about the booming sand dunes of the Asian desert. He wrote that the booming sands filled the air with the sounds of music, drums, and weapons of war. Booming sands are most often found in the middle of large deserts. They have been discovered all over the world, including the United States. Booming sands make loud, low-pitched sounds when the top layers of sand slip over the layers below, producing vibrations. The sounds have been compared to foghorns, cannon fire, and moaning. The sounds can last from a few seconds to 15 min and can be heard more than 10 km away!

_______ **1.** Which is a fact in this passage?
   A Marco Polo loved traveling.
   B Booming sands always sound like moaning people.
   C Booming sands are the most interesting thing in Asia.
   D Some booming sands are found in the United States.

_______ **2.** Which of the following phrases **best** describes booming sands?
   F found in Asia
   G noisy
   H slippery
   I discovered by Marco Polo

_______ **3.** What causes booming sands?
   A vibrations caused by top layers of sand slipping over layers below
   B battles in the desert
   C animals that live beneath sand dunes
   D There is not enough information to determine the answer.

Copyright © by Holt, Rinehart and Winston. All rights reserved.

Standardized Test Preparation *continued*

Passage 2 People who work in the field of architectural acoustics are concerned with controlling sound that travels in a closed space. Their goal is to make rooms and buildings quiet yet suitable for people to enjoy talking and listening to music. One major factor that affects the acoustical quality of a room is the way the room reflects sound waves. Sound waves bounce off surfaces such as doors, ceilings, and walls. Using materials that absorb sound reduces the reflection of sound waves. Materials that have small pockets of air that can trap the sound vibrations and keep them from reflecting are the most sound absorbent. Sound-absorbing floor and ceiling tiles, curtains, and upholstered furniture all help to control the reflection of sound waves.

_______ **1.** The field of architectural acoustics is concerned with which of the following?
    A making buildings earthquake safe
    B controlling sound in closed spaces
    C designing sound-absorbing materials
    D making buildings as quiet as possible

_______ **2.** Which of the following is a major factor in the acoustical quality of a room?
    F the size of the room
    G the furnishings in the room
    H the walls of the room
    I the noise level in the room

_______ **3.** Which of the following materials is **most** likely to absorb sounds the best?
    A materials that have small pockets of air
    B surfaces such as doors, ceilings, and walls
    C materials that keep the room as quiet as possible
    D furniture that is made of wood

Copyright © by Holt, Rinehart and Winston. All rights reserved.

Standardized Test Preparation *continued*

INTERPRETING GRAPHICS

Use the pictures of standing waves below to answer the questions that follow.

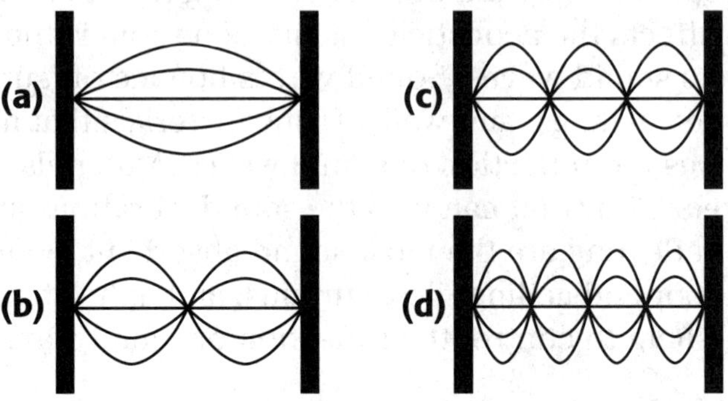

_______ **1.** Which of the standing waves has the lowest frequency?

    A a

    B b

    C c

    D d

_______ **2.** Which of the standing waves has the highest frequency?

    F a

    G b

    H c

    I d

_______ **3.** Which of the standing waves represents the first overtone?

    A a

    B b

    C c

    D d

_______ **4.** In which of the following pairs of standing waves is the frequency of the second wave twice the frequency of the first?

    F a, b

    G a, c

    H b, c

    I c, d

Copyright © by Holt, Rinehart and Winston. All rights reserved.

Standardized Test Preparation *continued*

MATH

Read each question below, and choose the best answer

______ **1.** The speed of sound in copper is 3,560 m/s. Which is another way to
express this measure?
A 356×10^2 m/s
B 0.356×10^3 m/s
C 3.56×10^3 m/s
D 3.56×10^4 m/s

______ **2.** The speed of sound in sea water is 1,522 m/s. How far can a sound
wave travel underwater in 10 s?
F 152.2 m
G 1,522 m
H 15,220 m
I 152,220 m

______ **3.** Claire likes to go swimming after work. She warms up for 120 s before
she begins swimming, and it takes her an average of 55 s to swim one
lap. Which equation could be used to find w, the number of seconds it
takes for Claire to warm up and swim 15 laps?
A $w = (15 \times 120) + 55$
B $w = (15 \times 55) + 120$
C $w = 120 + 55 + 15$
D $w = (15 \times 55) \times 120$

______ **4.** The Vasquez family went bowling. They rented 6 pairs of shoes for $3 a
pair and bowled for 2 h at a rate of $8.80/h. Which is the best estimate
of the total cost of the shoes and bowling?
F $24
G $30
H $36
I $45

Copyright © by Holt, Rinehart and Winston. All rights reserved.

Skills Practice Lab

Easy Listening

Pitch describes how low or high a sound is. A sound's pitch is related to its frequency—the number of waves per second. Frequency is measured in hertz (Hz), where 1 Hz equals 1 wave per second. Most humans can hear frequencies in the range from 20 Hz to 20,000 Hz. But not everyone detects all pitches equally well at all distances. In this activity, you will collect data to see how well you and your classmates hear different frequencies at different distances.

OBJECTIVES

Measure your classmates' ability to detect different pitches at different distances.

Graph the average class data.

Form a conclusion about how easily pitches of different frequencies are heard at different distances.

MATERIALS

- eraser, hard rubber
- meterstick
- paper, graph
- tuning forks, different frequencies (4)

ASK A QUESTION

1. Do most of the students in your classroom hear low-, mid-, or high-frequency sounds best?

FORM A HYPOTHESIS

2. Write a hypothesis that answers the question above. Explain your reasoning.

____

____

____

____

TEST THE HYPOTHESIS

3. Choose one member of your group to be the sound maker. The others will be the listeners.

Copyright © by Holt, Rinehart and Winston. All rights reserved.

Easy Listening *continued*

4. Use the data table below to record your data. Be sure to include a column for every listener in your group.

Data Collection Table

Frequency	Distance (m)			
	Listener 1	Listener 2	Listener 3	Average
1 (______Hz)				
2 (______Hz)				
3 (______Hz)				
4 (______Hz)				

5. The sound maker will choose one of the tuning forks, and record the frequency of the tuning fork in the data table.

6. The listeners should stand 1 m from the sound maker with their backs turned.

7. The sound maker will create a sound by striking the tip of the tuning fork gently with the eraser.

8. Listeners who hear the sound should take one step away from the sound maker. The listeners who do not hear the sound should stay where they are.

9. Repeat steps 7 and 8 until none of the listeners can hear the sound or the listeners reach the edge of the room.

10. Using the meterstick, the sound maker should measure the distance from his or her position to each of the listeners. All group members should record this data.

11. Repeat steps 5 through 10 with a tuning fork of a different frequency.

12. Continue until all four tuning forks have been tested.

ANALYZE THE RESULTS

1. **Organizing Data** Calculate the average distance for each frequency. Share your group's data with the rest of the class to make a data table for the whole class.

____

____

____

2. **Analyzing Data** Calculate the average distance for each frequency for the class.

____

____

Copyright © by Holt, Rinehart and Winston. All rights reserved.

3. Constructing Graphs Make a graph of the class results, plotting average distance (y-axis) versus frequency (x-axis).

DRAW CONCLUSIONS

4. Drawing Conclusions Was everyone in the class able to hear all of frequencies equally? (Hint: Was the average distance for each frequency the same?)

____

____

5. Evaluating Data If the answer to question 4 is no, which frequency had the longest average distance? Which frequency had the shortest final distance?

____

____

6. Analyzing Graphs Based on your graph, do your results support your hypothesis? Explain your answer.

____

____

7. Evaluating Methods Do you think your class sample is large enough to confirm your hypothesis for all people of all ages? Explain your answer.

____

____

____

____

Copyright © by Holt, Rinehart and Winston. All rights reserved.

Quick Lab **DATASHEET FOR QUICK LAB**

Good Vibrations

MATERIALS

- tuning fork
- rubber eraser
- small plastic cup of water

PROCEDURES

1. Gently strike a **tuning fork** on a **rubber eraser.** Watch the prongs, and listen for a sound. Describe what you see and hear.

____

____

____

2. Lightly touch the fork with your fingers. What do you feel?

____

____

3. Grasp the prongs of the fork firmly with your hand. What happens to the sound?

____

____

4. Strike the tuning fork on the eraser again, and dip the prongs in a **cup of water.** Describe what happens to the water.

____

____

____

Copyright © by Holt, Rinehart and Winston. All rights reserved.

Quick Lab

Sounding Board

MATERIALS

- desk
- ruler

SAFETY INFORMATION 

Be sure to wear safety goggles when doing this lab.

PROCEDURE

1. With one hand, hold a **ruler** on your **desk** so that one end of it hangs over the edge.

2. With your other hand, pull the free end of the ruler up a few centimeters, and let go.

3. Try pulling the ruler up different distances. How does the distance affect the sounds you hear? What property of the sound wave are you changing?

____

____

____

____

4. Change the length of the part that hangs over the edge. What property of the sound wave is affected? Record your answers and observations.

____

____

____

____

____

Copyright © by Holt, Rinehart and Winston. All rights reserved.

Inquiry Lab

The Speed of Sound

In the chapter entitled "The Nature of Sound," you learned that the speed of sound in air is 343 m/s at 20°C (approximately room temperature). In this lab, you'll design an experiment to measure the speed of sound yourself—and you'll determine if you're "up to speed"!

MATERIALS

- items to be determined by the students and approved by the teacher

PROCEDURE

1. Brainstorm with your teammates to come up with a way to measure the speed of sound. Consider the following as you design your experiment:

   a. You must have a method of making a sound. Some simple examples include speaking, clapping your hands, and hitting two boards together.

   b. Remember that speed is equal to distance divided by time. You must devise methods to measure the distance that a sound travels and to measure the amount of time it takes for that sound to travel that distance.

   c. Sound travels very rapidly. A sound from across the room will reach your ears almost before you can start recording the time! You may wish to have the sound travel a long distance.

   d. Remember that sound travels in waves. Think about the interactions of sound waves. You might be able to include these interactions in your design.

2. Discuss your experimental design with your teacher, including any equipment you need. Your teacher may have questions that will help you improve your design.

3. Once your design is approved, carry out your experiment. Be sure to perform several trials. Record your results.

ANALYZE THE RESULTS

1. Was your result close to the value given in the introduction to this lab? If not, what factors may have caused you to get such a different value?

   ____

   ____

   ____

   ____

Copyright © by Holt, Rinehart and Winston. All rights reserved.

The Speed of Sound *continued*

2. Why was it important for you to perform several trials in your experiment?

____

____

____

DRAW CONCLUSIONS

3. Compare your results with those of your classmates. Determine which experimental design provided the best results. Explain why you think this design was so successful.

____

____

____

Copyright © by Holt, Rinehart and Winston. All rights reserved.

Skills Practice Lab

DATASHEET FOR LABBOOK

Tuneful Tube

If you have seen a singer shatter a crystal glass simply by singing a note, you have seen an example of resonance. For the glass to shatter, the note has to match the resonant frequency of the glass. A column of air within a cylinder can also resonate if the air column is the proper length for the frequency of the note. In this lab, you will investigate the relationship between the length of an air column, the frequency, and the wavelength during resonance.

MATERIALS

- eraser, pink, rubber
- graduated cylinder, 100 mL
- paper, graph
- ruler, metric

- plastic tube, supplied by your teacher
- tuning forks, different frequencies (4)
- water

SAFETY INFORMATION 

PROCEDURE

1. Use the data table below to record your observations.

Data Collection Table				
Frequency (Hz)				
Length (cm)				

2. Fill the graduated cylinder with water.

3. Hold a plastic tube in the water so that about 3 cm is above the water.

4. Record the frequency of the first tuning fork. Gently strike the tuning fork with the eraser, and hold the tuning fork so that the prongs are just above the tube. Slowly move the tube and fork up and down until you hear the loudest sound.

5. Measure the distance from the top of the tube to the water. Record this length in your data table.

6. Repeat steps 3–5 using the other three tuning forks.

Copyright © by Holt, Rinehart and Winston. All rights reserved.

Tuneful Tube *continued*

ANALYZE THE RESULTS

1. Calculate the wavelength (in centimeters) of each sound wave by dividing the speed of sound in air (343 m/s at 20°C) by the frequency and multiplying by 100.

2. Make the following graphs: air column length versus frequency and wavelength versus frequency. On both graphs, plot the frequency on the x-axis.

3. Describe the trend between the length of the air column and the frequency of the tuning fork.

____

____

____

____

4. How are the pitches you heard related to the wavelengths of the sounds?

____

____

____

____

Copyright © by Holt, Rinehart and Winston. All rights reserved.

The Energy of Sound

In the chapter entitled "The Nature of Sound," you learned about various properties and interactions of sound. In this lab, you will perform several activities that will demonstrate that the properties and interactions of sound all depend on one thing—the energy carried by sound waves.

MATERIALS

- cup, plastic, small, filled with water
- eraser, pink, rubber
- rubber band
- string, 50 cm
- tuning forks, same frequency (2), different frequency (1)

SAFETY INFORMATION 

Part A: Sound Vibrations

PROCEDURE

1. Lightly strike a tuning fork with the eraser. Slowly place the prongs of the tuning fork in the plastic cup of water. Record your observations.

Part B: Resonance

PROCEDURE

1. Strike a tuning fork with the eraser. Quickly pick up a second tuning fork in your other hand, and hold it about 30 cm from the first tuning fork.

2. Place the first tuning fork against your leg to stop the tuning fork's vibration. Listen closely to the second tuning fork. Record your observations, including the frequencies of the two tuning forks.

____

____

3. Repeat steps 1 and 2, using the remaining tuning fork as the second tuning fork.

____

____

____

Copyright © by Holt, Rinehart and Winston. All rights reserved.

The Energy of Sound *continued*

Part C: Interference
PROCEDURE

1. Use the two tuning forks that have the same frequency, and place a rubber band tightly over the prongs near the base of one tuning fork. Strike both tuning forks against the eraser. Hold the stems of the tuning forks against a table, 3 cm to 5 cm apart. If you cannot hear any differences, move the rubber band up or down the prongs. Strike again. Record your observations.

____

____

Part D: The Doppler Effect
PROCEDURE

1. Your teacher will tie the piece of string securely to the base of one tuning fork. Your teacher will then strike the tuning fork and carefully swing the tuning fork in a circle overhead. Record your observations.

____

____

____

ANALYZE THE RESULTS

1. How do your observations demonstrate that sound waves are carried through vibrations?

____

____

2. Explain why you can hear a sound from the second tuning fork when the frequencies of the tuning forks used are the same.

____

____

____

____

____

Copyright © by Holt, Rinehart and Winston. All rights reserved.

The Energy of Sound *continued*

3. When using tuning forks of different frequencies, would you expect to hear a sound from the second tuning fork if you strike the first tuning fork harder? Explain your reasoning.

____

____

____

____

4. Did you notice the sound changing back and forth between loud and soft? A steady pattern like this one is called a *beat frequency*. Explain this changing pattern of loudness and softness in terms of interference (both constructive and destructive).

____

____

____

____

____

5. Did the tuning fork make a different sound when your teacher was swinging it than when he or she was holding it? If yes, explain why.

____

____

____

____

____

Copyright © by Holt, Rinehart and Winston. All rights reserved.

6. Is the actual pitch of the tuning fork changing when it is swinging? Explain.

____

____

____

____

____

DRAW CONCLUSIONS

7. Explain how your observations from each part of this lab verify that sound waves carry energy from one point to another through a vibrating medium.

____

____

____

____

____

____

____

8. Particularly loud thunder can cause the windows of your room to rattle. How is this evidence that sound waves carry energy?

____

____

____

____

____

Copyright © by Holt, Rinehart and Winston. All rights reserved.

Name _________________________________ Class _______________ Date _____________

Vocabulary Activity

Sound Puzzle

After you finish reading the chapter, give this puzzle a try! Fill in each blank with the correct term. Two blanks indicates a two-word term. Then use the vocabulary words to find the words in the puzzle on the next page.

1. The apparent change in the pitch of a car's horn as it moves past you is a

   result of the _________________________ _________________________.

2. When any kind of wave bounces off a barrier, the bouncing back of the

   wave is called _________________________.

3. A bounced sound wave is called a(n) _________________________.

4. Reflected sound waves are the basis for _________________________, a method
   whales and bats use to find food.

5. A longitudinal wave that is caused by vibrations and is carried through a

   medium is a(n) _________________________ _________________________.

6. Each instrument has a unique _________________________

   _________________________ that is the result of several pitches blending
   together through interference.

7. The extent to which a note can be heard determines its

   _________________________, and the _________________________ is how low or
   high the note sounds.

8. Due to _________________________, the vibration of a tuning fork can cause a
   guitar string to vibrate when the fork is held near the string.

9. The hammer, anvil, and stirrup bones are in the _________________________ ear.

10. Vibrations are changed into electrical signals in the

    _________________________ ear.

11. The part of the ear that collects sound waves is the _________________________
    ear.

12. Constructive or destructive _________________________ occurs when sound
    waves overlap and combine.

13. A unit used to express loudness of a sound is _________________________.

Copyright © by Holt, Rinehart and Winston. All rights reserved.

Vocabulary Activity *continued*

14. A nonmusical sound that includes a random mix of pitches is

_______________________.

15. An extremely fast airplane can cause an explosive sound called a(n)

_______________ _______________.

16. In a(n) _______________ _______________, some portions
of the wave are at rest while other portions have a large amplitude.

17. A physical environment in which phenomena occur is a(n)

_______________.

Search the puzzle below to find each of the words you wrote in the blanks above, and circle these words in the puzzle. The words for two-word terms will be found separately. Words may appear horizontally, vertically, or diagonally.

F	B	O	E	F	F	E	C	T	I	I	Z	E	W
I	Q	U	A	L	I	T	Y	M	N	R	R	C	A
W	G	T	D	T	O	T	W	F	T	M	E	H	V
V	B	E	W	R	K	U	R	L	E	V	L	O	E
R	U	R	X	A	E	A	D	Z	R	S	P	L	B
X	E	M	E	D	I	U	M	N	F	U	P	O	O
E	L	N	Z	O	K	C	C	E	E	N	O	C	O
F	D	O	N	N	O	I	S	E	R	S	D	A	M
J	E	I	H	I	O	K	C	Z	E	K	S	T	I
C	C	S	O	U	N	D	Y	H	N	X	Y	I	O
M	I	N	R	R	E	F	L	E	C	T	I	O	N
C	B	N	E	M	I	D	D	L	E	T	Y	N	I
R	E	S	O	N	A	N	C	E	Q	U	I	A	O
P	L	O	E	S	T	A	N	D	I	N	G	P	G

Copyright © by Holt, Rinehart and Winston. All rights reserved.

Name _______________________________ Class _______________ Date _____________

SciLinks Activity

WHAT IS SOUND?

Go to www.scilinks.org. To find links related to What Is Sound?, type in the keywords HSM1663. Then, use the links to answer the following questions about echolocation in bats.

Topic: What Is Sound?
SciLinks code: HSM1663
Go to www.scilinks.org

1. Find four new facts about echolocation in bats and record them here.

   a.____

   b.____

   c.____

   d.____

2. Now imagine that you have been given a bat detector. The bat detector picks up the bat calls on a microphone and creates a sound that is within human range of hearing. The frequency of the sound is directly related to the frequency of the sound the bat is making. Using the information you listed above, write a short story about your experiences listening to bats.

   ____

   ____

   ____

   ____

   ____

   ____

   ____

   ____

Copyright © by Holt, Rinehart and Winston. All rights reserved.

Performance-Based Assessment

Teacher Notes and Answer Key

PURPOSE

Students will demonstrate differences in the way sound reflects off of various surfaces and will use this information to investigate a real-life application.

TIME REQUIRED

One 45-minute class period. Students will need 20 minutes to perform the procedure and 25 minutes to answer the analysis questions.

RATING

Easy ← 1 2 3 4 → Hard

Teacher Prep–2
Student Set-Up–2
Concept Level–2
Clean Up–2

ADVANCE PREPARATION

Equip each activity station with the necessary materials. Plastic tubes of the same dimensions may be substituted for cardboard tubes. If enough clocks are not available, use a metronome or have students click two pencils together to provide a ticking sound. You may substitute a bath towel for the terry cloth.

SAFETY INFORMATION

Conduct this activity in a clear area, away from excess materials.

TEACHING STRATEGIES

This activity works best in groups of 2–3 students. Conduct this activity after reviewing Section: Interaction of Sound Waves. In order for the activity to work, the cardboard tubes cannot be touching and must be placed at an angle to each other. Also, advise students to speak in a quiet whisper so there is not a lot of outside noise affecting their observations.

Copyright © by Holt, Rinehart and Winston. All rights reserved.

Performance-Based Assessment *continued*

Evaluation Strategies

Use the following rubric to help evaluate student performance.

Rubric for Assessment

Possible points	Appropriate use of materials and equipment (30 points possible)
30–20	Task is complete; safe and careful handling of materials and equipment; attention to detail; superior lab skills
19–10	Task is generally complete; successful use of materials and equipment; somewhat unfocused performance
9–1	Task is incomplete; yields inadequate results; apparent lack of skill in handling materials and equipment
	Quality and clarity of observations (30 points possible)
30–20	Accurate observations stated clearly; good level of detail
19–10	Complete observations with some inaccuracies; moderate level of detail
9–1	Inaccurate, incomplete, or unclear observations; lack of detail
	Explanation of observations (40 points possible)
40–30	Clear, detailed explanation that shows superior understanding of the way sound waves reflect off various surfaces
29–20	Above-average explanation that shows good understanding of the way sound waves reflect off various surfaces
19–10	Adequate explanation that shows simple understanding of the way sound waves reflect off various surfaces; minor difficulty in expression
9–1	Lack of understanding of connection between observations and how sound waves reflect off various surfaces

Copyright © by Holt, Rinehart and Winston. All rights reserved.

Name _______________________________ Class _______________ Date _______________

Assessment   **SKILL BUILDER**

Performance-Based Assessment

OBJECTIVE

You will demonstrate differences in the way sound reflects off of various surfaces and use this information to investigate a real-life application.

KNOW THE SCORE!

As you work through the activity, keep in mind that you will be earning a grade for the following:

- how well you work with materials and equipment (30%)
- how well you state your observations (30%)
- how well you use your observations to answer analysis questions (40%)

MATERIALS AND EQUIPMENT

- table (at least 1.5 m long and 1 m wide)
- metric ruler
- 40 × 40 cm of poster board
- masking tape

- 2 cardboard tubes (each 50 cm long, 5 cm in diameter)
- clock that ticks
- 40 × 40 cm of terry cloth or bath towel
- 40 × 40 × 5 cm of foam rubber

Using Scientific Methods

ASK A QUESTION

How does sound respond when it hits different materials?

FORM A HYPOTHESIS

1. Your station has three different materials: poster board, terry cloth, and foam rubber. Which do you think will reflect sound the best? Which will absorb the most sound?

   Poster board will reflect sound the best. Foam rubber will absorb sound the most.

Material	What I hear
Poster board	I clearly hear the ticking of the clock.
Terry cloth	I can still hear the ticking of the clock, but it is quieter.
Foam rubber	I can still hear the ticking of the clock, but it is even more muffled than with the terry cloth

Copyright © by Holt, Rinehart and Winston. All rights reserved.

Name _________________________________ Class _______________ Date _____________

Performance-Based Assessment *continued*

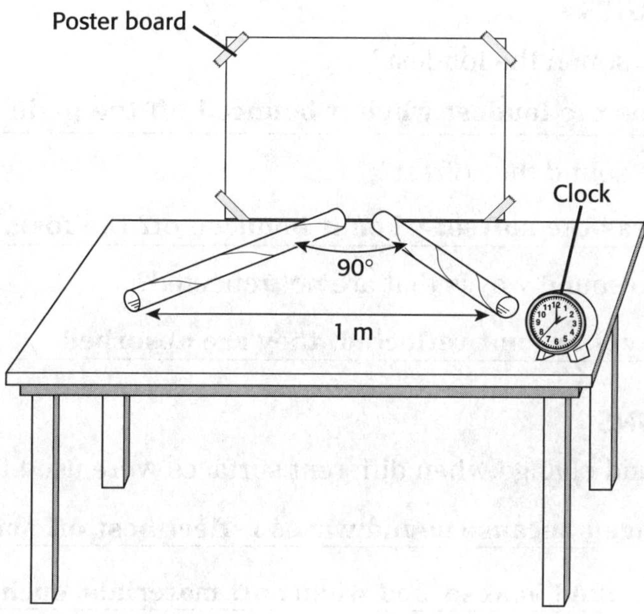

TEST THE HYPOTHESIS

2. Place the table 5 cm away from a wall.

3. Tape the poster board securely to the wall over the center of the table.

4. Place the cardboard tubes on the table so that one edge of each tube is approximately 5 cm from the poster board.

5. Arrange the cardboard tubes so that the ends that are closest to the poster board create a 90° angle to each other. The cardboard tubes should not touch each other.

6. The ends of the cardboard tubes that are farthest away from the poster board should be approximately 1 m apart.

7. Place the clock near the end of one of the cardboard tubes. You will be listening for the clock at the end of the other cardboard tube. The clock should be placed at the end of the cardboard tube that is farthest away from the poster board.

8. Check your setup by looking at the picture. Make any necessary changes.

9. Listen through the cardboard tube which does not have the clock in front of it. Make sure you hear it ticking. If you cannot hear the clock, adjust your setup.

10. Cover one ear, and put your other ear against the tube that is not next to the clock. Record the sound you hear in the table above.

11. Place the piece of terry cloth over the poster board. Repeat step 10, and record your observations.

12. Remove the fabric, and replace it with the piece of foam rubber. Repeat step 10 and record your observations.

Copyright © by Holt, Rinehart and Winston. All rights reserved.

Name _______________________________ Class _______________ Date _______________

Performance-Based Assessment *continued*

ANALYZE THE RESULTS

13. a. When was the sound the loudest?

The sound was the loudest when it bounced off the plain poster board.

b. When was the sound the softest?

The sound was the softest when it bounced off the foam rubber.

14. What happens to sound waves that are not reflected?

When sound waves are not reflected, they are absorbed.

DRAW CONCLUSIONS

15. Why did the sound change when different surfaces were used for reflection?

The sound changed because sound waves reflect best off smooth, hard

surfaces. More sound is absorbed when soft materials, such as foam

rubber, are used.

16. a. Concert halls are difficult to design because the designer must use both reflective and absorptive surfaces in order to achieve the best sound. What type of material would you use to reflect sound in a concert hall? Explain your answer.

I would use a hard surface to reflect sound because the poster board

reflected sound better than the softer terry cloth and foam rubber.

b. What type of material would you use to absorb sound in a concert hall?

I would use foam rubber because it produced the most muffled sound

of the three materials I used. This means it absorbed the most sound

of the three materials.

17. a. Why would you not want to use all soft materials inside a concert hall?

Too much sound would be absorbed by the soft material, so some

people would not be able to hear the concert.

b. Why would you not want to use all hard materials inside a concert hall?

Too much sound would be reflected by the hard surfaces. This would

create echoes and uncontrolled sound reflection in the concert hall.

Copyright © by Holt, Rinehart and Winston. All rights reserved.

Skills Practice Lab

DATASHEET FOR CHAPTER LAB

Easy Listening

Teacher Notes and Answer Key

TIME REQUIRED

One or two 45-minute class periods

RATING

Teacher Prep–1
Student Set-Up–1
Concept Level–2
Clean Up–1

MATERIALS

For each group of 3 to 4 students:

- 4 tuning forks of different frequencies
- pink rubber eraser (or tuning fork mallet)
- meterstick
- graph paper

LAB NOTES

You may wish to use the classroom graph to have students practice interpreting a graph. For instance, you could ask students to try and pinpoint the distances at which other frequencies might be heard based on the graph.

Copyright © by Holt, Rinehart and Winston. All rights reserved.

Name _______________________ Class _______________ Date __________

Skills Practice Lab **DATASHEET FOR CHAPTER LAB**

Easy Listening

Pitch describes how low or high a sound is. A sound's pitch is related to its frequency—the number of waves per second. Frequency is measured in hertz (Hz), where 1 Hz equals 1 wave per second. Most humans can hear frequencies in the range from 20 Hz to 20,000 Hz. But not everyone detects all pitches equally well at all distances. In this activity, you will collect data to see how well you and your classmates hear different frequencies at different distances.

OBJECTIVES

Measure your classmates' ability to detect different pitches at different distances.

Graph the average class data.

Form a conclusion about how easily pitches of different frequencies are heard at different distances.

MATERIALS

- eraser, hard rubber
- meterstick
- paper, graph
- tuning forks, different frequencies (4)

ASK A QUESTION

1. Do most of the students in your classroom hear low-, mid-, or high-frequency sounds best?

FORM A HYPOTHESIS

2. Write a hypothesis that answers the question above. Explain your reasoning.

Sample answer: Most of the students in the class will hear mid-frequency

sounds better. (accept any testable hypothesis)

____

____

TEST THE HYPOTHESIS

3. Choose one member of your group to be the sound maker. The others will be the listeners.

Copyright © by Holt, Rinehart and Winston. All rights reserved.

Name _________________________________ Class _______________ Date _____________

Easy Listening *continued*

4. Use the data table below to record your data. Be sure to include a column for every listener in your group.

Data Collection Table				
	Distance (m)			
Frequency	Listener 1	Listener 2	Listener 3	Average
1 (_____Hz)				
2 (_____Hz)				
3 (_____Hz)				
4 (_____Hz)				

5. The sound maker will choose one of the tuning forks, and record the frequency of the tuning fork in the data table.

6. The listeners should stand 1 m from the sound maker with their backs turned.

7. The sound maker will create a sound by striking the tip of the tuning fork gently with the eraser.

8. Listeners who hear the sound should take one step away from the sound maker. The listeners who do not hear the sound should stay where they are.

9. Repeat steps 7 and 8 until none of the listeners can hear the sound or the listeners reach the edge of the room.

10. Using the meterstick, the sound maker should measure the distance from his or her position to each of the listeners. All group members should record this data.

11. Repeat steps 5 through 10 with a tuning fork of a different frequency.

12. Continue until all four tuning forks have been tested.

ANALYZE THE RESULTS

1. Organizing Data Calculate the average distance for each frequency. Share your group's data with the rest of the class to make a data table for the whole class.

You may wish to provide a table on the board or on an overhead transparency for students to record their data. The table should include a column for each group and a row for the distance measurement for each tuning fork.

2. Analyzing Data Calculate the average distance for each frequency for the class.

Calculate the class average for each frequency. All students should have the same averages.

Copyright © by Holt, Rinehart and Winston. All rights reserved.

Name _________________________________ Class _______________ Date _____________

Easy Listening *continued*

3. Constructing Graphs Make a graph of the class results, plotting average distance (*y*-axis) versus frequency (*x*-axis).

The graph will vary depending on what frequencies are used, surrounding noise levels, and individual hearing abilities. See the sample graph:

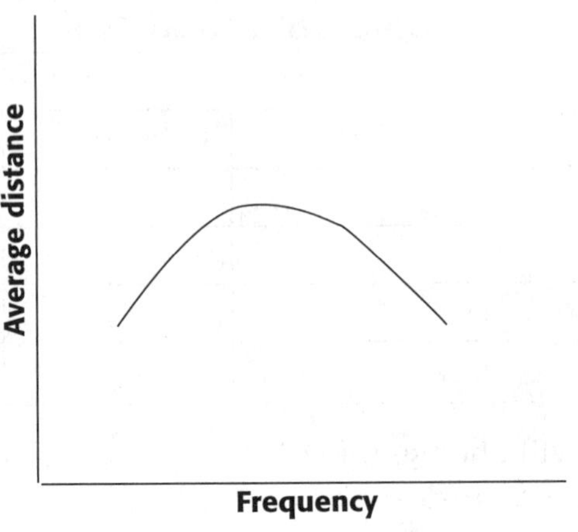

DRAW CONCLUSIONS

4. Drawing Conclusions Was everyone in the class able to hear all of frequencies equally? (Hint: Was the average distance for each frequency the same?)

The average distance for each frequency should be different.

5. Evaluating Data If the answer to question 4 is no, which frequency had the longest average distance? Which frequency had the shortest final distance?

Answers will depend on which frequencies were used. Accept all answers

that agree with class data.

6. Analyzing Graphs Based on your graph, do your results support your hypothesis? Explain your answer.

Answers will vary depending on hypotheses. Accept all reasonable responses.

7. Evaluating Methods Do you think your class sample is large enough to confirm your hypothesis for all people of all ages? Explain your answer.

The class sample is not enough to confirm the hypothesis for all humans of

all ages, because most people in the classroom are the same age. In addition,

the number of students in an average classroom is just too small to provide

results that can be extended to the general population.

Copyright © by Holt, Rinehart and Winston. All rights reserved.

Name _______________________________ Class _________________ Date _________

Quick Lab

DATASHEET FOR QUICK LAB

Good Vibrations

MATERIALS

- tuning fork
- rubber eraser
- small plastic cup of water

PROCEDURES

1. Gently strike a **tuning fork** on a **rubber eraser.** Watch the prongs, and listen for a sound. Describe what you see and hear.

Students should hear a faint sound coming from the tuning fork. They may or

may not see the prongs of the tuning fork vibrate—this will depend on how

hard the fork was struck and on the size of the fork.

2. Lightly touch the fork with your fingers. What do you feel?

Students should feel that the prongs are vibrating.

3. Grasp the prongs of the fork firmly with your hand. What happens to the sound?

After the students grasp the prongs, the sound will immediately stop.

4. Strike the tuning fork on the eraser again, and dip the prongs in a **cup of water.** Describe what happens to the water.

The vibrations of the prongs will create waves in the water in the cup.

Safety Caution: Remind students that the tuning forks should not touch their eyes or eyeglasses.

Copyright © by Holt, Rinehart and Winston. All rights reserved.

Name _______________________________ Class _______________ Date ____________

Quick Lab) **DATASHEET FOR QUICK LAB**

Sounding Board

MATERIALS

- desk
- ruler

SAFETY INFORMATION 

Be sure to wear safety goggles when doing this lab.

PROCEDURE

1. With one hand, hold a **ruler** on your **desk** so that one end of it hangs over the edge.

2. With your other hand, pull the free end of the ruler up a few centimeters, and let go.

3. Try pulling the ruler up different distances. How does the distance affect the sounds you hear? What property of the sound wave are you changing?

The farther up they pull the ruler, the louder the sound will be. Amplitude is

changing.

____

____

4. Change the length of the part that hangs over the edge. What property of the sound wave is affected? Record your answers and observations.

The shorter the length of the ruler hanging off the edge of the table, the

higher the pitch will be. Changing the length of the ruler hanging off the

edge changes the frequency of the sound wave.

____

____

Safety Caution: Remind student to wear safety goggles when doing this lab.

Teacher's Notes: Any stiff wooden or plastic ruler will work for this lab.

Copyright © by Holt, Rinehart and Winston. All rights reserved.

DATASHEET FOR LABBOOK

The Speed of Sound

Teacher Notes and Answer Key

Paul Boyle
Perry Heights Middle School
Evansville, Indiana

TIME REQUIRED

One 45-minute class period

RATING

Easy ←—— 1   2   3   4 —→ Hard

Teacher Prep–2
Student Set-Up–2
Concept Level–2
Clean Up–1

MATERIALS

Students will need stopwatches, measuring tapes, and various types of noisemakers (cymbals, wood blocks, drums, horns, and so on). You will need an area where students can hear an echo. A long hall will do, but this lab generally works better outside. To make this lab even more interesting, you might have a contest with awards for the most creative experiment, the most accurate experiment, and the experiment with the least spread in the data for multiple measurements.

SAFETY CAUTION

Be sure that you have approved all experimental designs before students proceed.

Copyright © by Holt, Rinehart and Winston. All rights reserved.

Name _______________________________ Class ________________ Date ____________

Inquiry Lab

DATASHEET FOR LABBOOK

The Speed of Sound

In the chapter entitled "The Nature of Sound," you learned that the speed of sound in air is 343 m/s at 20°C (approximately room temperature). In this lab, you'll design an experiment to measure the speed of sound yourself—and you'll determine if you're "up to speed"!

MATERIALS

- items to be determined by the students and approved by the teacher

PROCEDURE

1. Brainstorm with your teammates to come up with a way to measure the speed of sound. Consider the following as you design your experiment:

   a. You must have a method of making a sound. Some simple examples include speaking, clapping your hands, and hitting two boards together.

   b. Remember that speed is equal to distance divided by time. You must devise methods to measure the distance that a sound travels and to measure the amount of time it takes for that sound to travel that distance.

   c. Sound travels very rapidly. A sound from across the room will reach your ears almost before you can start recording the time! You may wish to have the sound travel a long distance.

   d. Remember that sound travels in waves. Think about the interactions of sound waves. You might be able to include these interactions in your design.

2. Discuss your experimental design with your teacher, including any equipment you need. Your teacher may have questions that will help you improve your design.

3. Once your design is approved, carry out your experiment. Be sure to perform several trials. Record your results.

ANALYZE THE RESULTS

1. Was your result close to the value given in the introduction to this lab? If not, what factors may have caused you to get such a different value?

   Answers may vary. Factors that could cause a different value include air

   temperature and accuracy of distance and time measurements.

Copyright © by Holt, Rinehart and Winston. All rights reserved.

Name _________________________________ Class _______________ Date ____________

The Speed of Sound *continued*

2. Why was it important for you to perform several trials in your experiment?

Several trials are necessary in order to confirm results and to rule out the

possibility of reporting an error because just one measurement was used.

DRAW CONCLUSIONS

3. Compare your results with those of your classmates. Determine which experimental design provided the best results. Explain why you think this design was so successful.

Answers may vary. Accept all reasonable responses.

Copyright © by Holt, Rinehart and Winston. All rights reserved.

Skills Practice Lab

DATASHEET FOR LABBOOK

Tuneful Tube

Teacher Notes and Answer Key

TIME REQUIRED

One 45-minute class period

RATING

Easy ◄──── 1   2   3   4 ────► Hard

Teacher Prep–3
Student Set-Up–1
Concept Level–3
Clean Up–2

MATERIALS

The length of tube needed (PVC pipe works well) equals 25 times the speed of sound in air (343 m/s at 20°C) divided by the lowest frequency of the tuning forks used. (The answer is one-fourth the wavelength of the sound wave expressed in centimeters.) Cut each tube at least 5 cm longer than the calculated length. You may want to demonstrate the resonance point so students can hear the change in volume.

Copyright © by Holt, Rinehart and Winston. All rights reserved.

Name _______________________________ Class _______________ Date _____________

Skills Practice Lab

DATASHEET FOR LABBOOK

Tuneful Tube

If you have seen a singer shatter a crystal glass simply by singing a note, you have seen an example of resonance. For the glass to shatter, the note has to match the resonant frequency of the glass. A column of air within a cylinder can also resonate if the air column is the proper length for the frequency of the note. In this lab, you will investigate the relationship between the length of an air column, the frequency, and the wavelength during resonance.

MATERIALS

- eraser, pink, rubber
- graduated cylinder, 100 mL
- paper, graph
- ruler, metric
- plastic tube, supplied by your teacher
- tuning forks, different frequencies (4)
- water

SAFETY INFORMATION 

PROCEDURE

1. Use the data table below to record your observations.

Data Collection Table				
Frequency (Hz)				
Length (cm)				

2. Fill the graduated cylinder with water.

3. Hold a plastic tube in the water so that about 3 cm is above the water.

4. Record the frequency of the first tuning fork. Gently strike the tuning fork with the eraser, and hold the tuning fork so that the prongs are just above the tube. Slowly move the tube and fork up and down until you hear the loudest sound.

5. Measure the distance from the top of the tube to the water. Record this length in your data table.

6. Repeat steps 3–5 using the other three tuning forks.

Copyright © by Holt, Rinehart and Winston. All rights reserved.

Name _______________________________ Class ________________ Date ____________

Tuneful Tube *continued*

ANALYZE THE RESULTS

1. Calculate the wavelength (in centimeters) of each sound wave by dividing the speed of sound in air (343 m/s at 20°C) by the frequency and multiplying by 100.

Answers will depend on the frequency of the tuning forks.

2. Make the following graphs: air column length versus frequency and wavelength versus frequency. On both graphs, plot the frequency on the *x*-axis.

Graphs will depend on results. Sample graphs are shown.

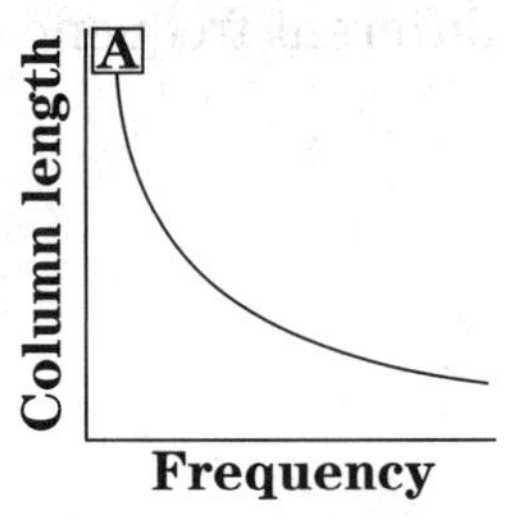

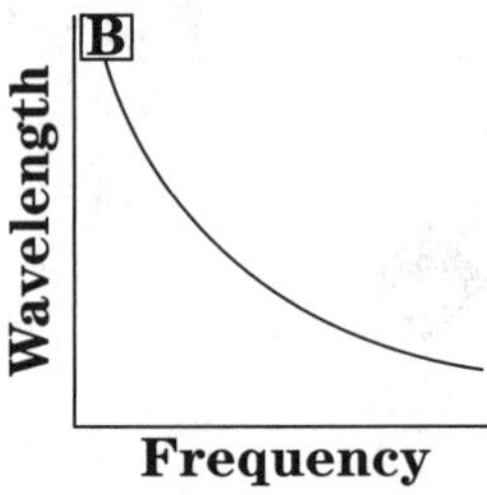

3. Describe the trend between the length of the air column and the frequency of the tuning fork.

As the frequency decreases, the length of the air column increases.

4. How are the pitches you heard related to the wavelengths of the sounds?

The pitches (which are determined by the frequencies) are inversely related

to the wavelengths of the sounds. As the pitch gets lower (when the

frequency decreases), the wavelength increases.

Copyright © by Holt, Rinehart and Winston. All rights reserved.

Skills Practice Lab)

DATASHEET FOR LABBOOK

The Energy of Sound

Kevin McCurdy
Elmwood Junior High
Rogers, Arkansas

Teacher Notes and Answer Key

TIME REQUIRED

One or two 45-minute class periods

RATING

Easy ◄——1———2———3———4——► Hard

Teacher Prep–2
Student Set-Up–1
Concept Level–4
Clean Up–1

SAFETY CAUTION

Make sure students are at a safe distance before you perform the Part D exercise.
You might wish to take the class outside.

Copyright © by Holt, Rinehart and Winston. All rights reserved.

Name _________________________________ Class _______________ Date _____________

Skills Practice Lab)   **DATASHEET FOR LABBOOK**

The Energy of Sound

In the chapter entitled "The Nature of Sound," you learned about various properties and interactions of sound. In this lab, you will perform several activities that will demonstrate that the properties and interactions of sound all depend on one thing—the energy carried by sound waves.

MATERIALS

- cup, plastic, small, filled with water
- eraser, pink, rubber
- rubber band
- string, 50 cm
- tuning forks, same frequency (2), different frequency (1)

SAFETY INFORMATION 

Part A: Sound Vibrations
PROCEDURE

1. Lightly strike a tuning fork with the eraser. Slowly place the prongs of the tuning fork in the plastic cup of water. Record your observations.

Part B: Resonance
PROCEDURE

1. Strike a tuning fork with the eraser. Quickly pick up a second tuning fork in your other hand, and hold it about 30 cm from the first tuning fork.

2. Place the first tuning fork against your leg to stop the tuning fork's vibration. Listen closely to the second tuning fork. Record your observations, including the frequencies of the two tuning forks.

____

____

3. Repeat steps 1 and 2, using the remaining tuning fork as the second tuning fork.

____

____

____

____

Copyright © by Holt, Rinehart and Winston. All rights reserved.

Name _________________________________ Class _______________ Date _________

The Energy of Sound *continued*

Part C: Interference
PROCEDURE

1. Use the two tuning forks that have the same frequency, and place a rubber band tightly over the prongs near the base of one tuning fork. Strike both tuning forks against the eraser. Hold the stems of the tuning forks against a table, 3 cm to 5 cm apart. If you cannot hear any differences, move the rubber band up or down the prongs. Strike again. Record your observations.

____

____

Part D: The Doppler Effect
PROCEDURE

1. Your teacher will tie the piece of string securely to the base of one tuning fork. Your teacher will then strike the tuning fork and carefully swing the tuning fork in a circle overhead. Record your observations.

____

____

ANALYZE THE RESULTS

1. How do your observations demonstrate that sound waves are carried through vibrations?

   In Part A, the water begins to move when the tuning fork is placed in the

   water. Vibrations from the tuning fork caused the water's movement.

2. Explain why you can hear a sound from the second tuning fork when the frequencies of the tuning forks used are the same.

   The vibrating tuning fork causes the air to vibrate at a certain frequency.

   The energy of the vibrations is transferred through the air to the second

   tuning fork, which starts to resonate (vibrate at the same frequency). This

   phenomenon happened in Part B.

____

Copyright © by Holt, Rinehart and Winston. All rights reserved.

Name _________________________________ Class _______________ Date _____________

The Energy of Sound *continued*

3. When using tuning forks of different frequencies, would you expect to hear a sound from the second tuning fork if you strike the first tuning fork harder? Explain your reasoning.

Hitting the first tuning fork harder causes a larger amount of energy to be

transferred from the tuning fork to the air. However, the vibration of the air

particles is not at the same frequency as the second tuning fork and will

therefore not cause the second tuning fork to make a sound.

4. Did you notice the sound changing back and forth between loud and soft? A steady pattern like this one is called a *beat frequency*. Explain this changing pattern of loudness and softness in terms of interference (both constructive and destructive).

The loudness corresponds to constructive interference (when the crests

of the sound waves overlap, increasing the amplitude), and the softness

corresponds to destructive interference (when the crests and troughs of

sound waves overlap, decreasing the amplitude). A beat frequency caused

by constructive and destructive interference could be heard in Part C.

5. Did the tuning fork make a different sound when your teacher was swinging it than when he or she was holding it? If yes, explain why.

yes; In Part D, as the tuning fork swings toward the listeners, the pitch

is higher because the sound waves in front of it are closer together and

therefore have a higher frequency. As the tuning fork swings away from the

listeners, the pitch is lower because the sound waves are farther apart and

therefore have a lower frequency.

Copyright © by Holt, Rinehart and Winston. All rights reserved.

Name _______________________________ Class _______________ Date ___________

The Energy of Sound *continued*

6. Is the actual pitch of the tuning fork changing when it is swinging? Explain.

yes; The pitch you hear in Part D changes because of the Doppler effect, but the actual frequency of the tuning fork does not change.

DRAW CONCLUSIONS

7. Explain how your observations from each part of this lab verify that sound waves carry energy from one point to another through a vibrating medium.

Part A shows that the vibrations of the tuning fork have energy that does work on the water. Part B shows that the energy from one vibrating tuning fork can be passed by vibrations through the air to cause another tuning fork to vibrate. Part C shows that the energy from each vibrating tuning fork can travel through the air as waves that can interfere with each other. Part D shows that the vibrations from a tuning fork travel through the air to your ears, and the amount of energy being carried by the vibration determines what is heard (higher pitch = higher frequency = higher energy).

8. Particularly loud thunder can cause the windows of your room to rattle. How is this evidence that sound waves carry energy?

It takes energy to move the windows to cause them to rattle. Therefore, energy from the thunder's sound waves must be transferred through the air to the windows.

Copyright © by Holt, Rinehart and Winston. All rights reserved.

Answer Key

Directed Reading A

SECTION: WHAT IS SOUND?

1. vibration
2. compression
3. rarefaction
4. sound waves
5. in all directions
6. Wind gusts from the speakers would knock people over.
7. medium
8. In a vacuum there are no particles to vibrate.
9. Sound needs a medium through which to travel. As the air is removed from the jar, the sound waves begin to disappear.
10. C
11. G
12. A
13. E
14. F
15. B
16. C
17. D
18. C
19. A
20. B
21. B
22. E
23. A
24. D
25. C
26. Vibrations in the tree and ground create compressions and rarefactions in the air.
27. A
28. B

SECTION: PROPERTIES OF SOUND

1. sound waves
2. B
3. As a medium cools, the speed of sound generally decreases.
4. They transmit energy more slowly.
5. He became the first person to travel faster than the speed of sound.
6. A
7. D
8. D
9. Doppler effect
10. The compressions and rarefactions are closer together than they would be if the sound source was not moving.
11. high
12. low
13. The driver always hears the same pitch.
14. A
15. B
16. C
17. An oscilloscope can graph representations of sound waves.
18. The graph on the right shows a sound with a lower frequency than the one on the left.
19. The sound represented on the right has a lower pitch than the one on the left.
20. The line on a graph from an oscilloscope represents the sound waves. The highest points are the compressions and the lowest points are the rarefactions.

SECTION: INTERACTIONS OF SOUND WAVES

1. They use sounds to communicate and to find food.
2. reflection
3. echo
4. one that is hard and smooth
5. echoes
6. echolocation
7. Because of the Doppler effect, the frequency of the echo tells the bat if the insect is flying toward it.
8. sonar
9. to locate objects underwater; to avoid icebergs; to map the ocean floor
10. ultrasonography
11. performing surgery without making an incision; monitoring the development of an unborn baby; examining internal organs

Copyright © by Holt, Rinehart and Winston. All rights reserved.

12. interference
13. destructive
14. constructive
15. sonic boom
16. When a jet flies faster than the speed of sound, the sound waves spread out behind it in a cone shape. The sound waves combine on the edge of the cone by constructive interference. This creates a shock wave, which you hear as a sonic boom.
17. standing wave
18. two objects naturally vibrating at the same frequency
19. when the resonant frequency of the tuning fork matches one of the resonant frequencies of the string.
20. An acoustic guitar has a hollow body. When the strings vibrate, sound waves enter the body of the guitar. Standing waves form inside the body of the guitar, and the sound is amplified.

SECTION: SOUND QUALITY

1. D
2. A single note on an instrument actually comes from several different pitches: the fundamental and several overtones.
3. sound quality
4. C
5. C
6. A
7. B
8. A
9. C
10. B
11. B
12. A
13. C
14. B
15. A
16. lower pitch
17. lower pitch
18. lower pitch
19. B
20. noise
21. Answers will vary. Sample answer: The first sound wave shows a repeating pattern. The second is noise and has no regular pattern.

Directed Reading B

SECTION: WHAT IS SOUND?

1. vibration
2. compression
3. rarefaction
4. sound wave
5. in all directions
6. C
7. medium
8. vacuum
9. B
10. C
11. A
12. D
13. B
14. B
15. B
16. D
17. A
18. D
19. B
20. A
21. B

SECTION: PROPERTIES OF SOUND

1. A	11. A
2. B	12. B
3. B	13. B
4. B	14. A
5. A	15. C
6. D	16. A
7. A	17. A
8. D	18. B
9. B	19. C
10. B	

SECTION: INTERACTIONS OF SOUND WAVES

1. A
2. C
3. reflection
4. echo
5. echolocation
6. Doppler effect
7. sonar
8. B
9. interference
10. destructive
11. constructive
12. sonic boom
13. B
14. B
15. C

Copyright © by Holt, Rinehart and Winston. All rights reserved.

16. B   **18.** D

17. A   **19.** D

SECTION: SOUND QUALITY

1. D   **7.** B

2. D   **8.** C

3. B   **9.** B

4. A   **10.** D

5. A   **11.** B

6. B   **12.** C

Vocabulary and Section Summary

SECTION: WHAT IS SOUND?

1. sound wave: a longitudinal wave that is caused by vibrations and that travels through a material medium

2. medium: a physical environment in which phenomena occur

SECTION: PROPERTIES OF SOUND

1. pitch: a measure of how high or low a sound is perceived to be, depending on the frequency of the sound wave

2. Doppler effect: an observed change in the frequency of a wave when the source or observer is moving

3. loudness: the extent to which a sound can be heard

4. decibel: the most common unit used to measure loudness (symbol, dB)

SECTION: INTERACTIONS OF SOUND WAVES

1. echo: a reflected sound wave

2. echolocation: the process of using reflected sound waves to find objects; used by animals such as bats

3. interference: the combination of two or more waves that results in a single wave

4. sonic boom: the explosive sound heard when a shock wave from an object traveling faster than the speed of sound reaches a person's ears

5. standing wave: a pattern of vibration that simulates a wave that is standing still

6. resonance: a phenomenon that occurs when two objects naturally vibrate at the same frequency; the sound produced by one object causes the other object to vibrate

SECTION: SOUND QUALITY

1. sound quality: the result of the blending of several pitches through interference

2. noise: a sound that consists of a random mix of frequencies

Section Review

SECTION: WHAT IS SOUND?

1. Answers will vary. Sample answer: A sound wave is carried through a medium by longitudinal waves.

2. B

3. C

4. Wearing ear protection devices, and keeping a distance between your ears and loud sounds.

5. All sounds are carried by longitudinal waves: in a wave, the particles themselves do not move forward.

6. No; there is no medium between the moon and Earth to carry sound waves.

7. The breaking of dishes involves a high energy of vibrations, so the sound is loud.

8. a longitudinal wave

9. Diagrams should label the areas dense with particles as compressions, and sparse areas rarefactions.

10. The back-and-forth motion of a vibrating object forms compressions and rarefactions in the air around it.

SECTION: PROPERTIES OF SOUND

1. Answers will vary. Sample answer: How low or high a sound seems, which depends on the frequency of the sound waves.

2. Loudness is expressed scientifically in units of decibels.

3. C

4. Sound tends to travel fastest in higher-temperature media.

5. Pitch is determined by the frequency of sound waves.

6. An oscilloscope changes sound waves into electronic signals, which are represented on a screen.

7. $343 \text{ m/s} \times 2 \text{ s} = 686 \text{ m}$

8. $1500 \text{ m/s} \times 4 \text{ s} = 6000 \text{ m}$

9. Yes; the sound waves in front of the source will become closer together as the source moves forward. Also, the

Copyright © by Holt, Rinehart and Winston. All rights reserved.

listener will "meet" the sound waves more rapidly by moving toward the source. The movements of both the source and the listener will make the pitch of the sound higher.

10. The amplitude of the sound will be higher when the drum is struck harder, but the frequency will not change.

SECTION: INTERACTIONS OF SOUND WAVES

1. Answers will vary. Sample answer: Some animals use echolocation to see in the dark by listening for the echoes of the sounds they make off reflected objects.
2. standing wave
3. resonance
4. A
5. Answers will vary. Sample answer: a room with smooth walls
6. They use echolocation to find insects by emitting sounds and listening for the echoes, which tell them how far away the insect is and how fast it is moving.
7. Answers will vary. Sample answer: constructive interference: sonic boom; destructive interference: a "dead spot" in a concert hall
8. 343 m/s $\times$ 0.05 s = 17 m
   17 m $\div$ 2 = 8.5 m
9. Resonance is occurring, because the lamp on top of the piano has a resonant frequency equal to one of the notes being played.
10. Both sonar and ultrasonography make use of sound reflection to locate objects. Ultrasonography, however, involves much higher-frequency sound waves than used in sonar, and allows imaging of objects instead of just locating them.

SECTION: SOUND QUALITY

1. Answers will vary. Sample answers: Each instrument has a different sound quality based on how it produces sound. Static from the TV or radio is an example of noise.
2. D
3. A musical instrument's particular shape and way of producing sound give it its unique sound quality.

4. String instruments and wind instruments both make standing waves, string instruments along the string and wind instruments inside the air column, to produce sound.
5. Probably not; people use the word "noise" in common speech to mean any unpleasant noise, which might be applied by someone to a particular kind of music even if that music is not merely a random mix of frequencies.
6. The sound is music. The oscilloscope shows an image of a wave with a repeating pattern.

Chapter Review

1. loudness
2. echoes
3. sound quality
4. A
5. D
6. C
7. C
8. D
9. B
10. A beluga whale emits high pitched noises, which reflect off the fish. If a fish is moving away from the whale, the echo off the fish that the whale hears will have a lower pitch than the original sound. If the fish is moving toward the whale, the echo off the fish heard by the whale will have a higher pitch than the original sound.
11. The back-and-forth motions of vibrations of an object cause compressions and rarefactions in the air around it, which is carried outward as sound waves.
12. In the outer ear, sound waves are funneled into the ear canal. In the middle ear, the hammer, anvil, and stirrup increase the size of the vibrations. In the inner ear, these vibrations are changed into electrical signals for the brain to interpret.
13. 1,500 m/s $\times$ 6 s = 9,000 m
    9,000 m $\div$ 2 = 4,500 m
14. An answer to this exercise can be found at the end of the teacher's edition.
15. This design eliminates echoes because the surfaces of the walls absorb sound waves instead of reflecting them.

Copyright © by Holt, Rinehart and Winston. All rights reserved.

16. No; a sonic boom is only audible to an observer behind the plane along the shock wave. Once the airplane breaks the sound barrier, the plane outruns the sonic boom, so the pilot does not hear it.

17. The worker may be suffering from tinnitus, caused by long exposure to loud sounds. Further hearing loss could be prevented by wearing hearing protection while on the job.

18. D

19. A

20. C

21. B, C

Reinforcement

DOPPLER DAN'S DUMP TRUCK

1. 343 m/s

2. (343 m/s) ÷ 350 Hz = 0.98 m

3. 0.90 m

4. (343 m/s) ÷ 0.90 m = 381 Hz

5. 1.06 m

6. (343 m/s) ÷ 1.06 m = 324 Hz

7. sound wavelength: 0.98 m, 0.90 m, 1.06 m; sound frequency: 350 Hz, 381 Hz, 324 Hz

8. As the dump truck moved toward Otis, he heard a higher frequency (higher pitched) sound than Dan. Dan was moving with the sound source, so he heard the actual frequency of the horn.

Critical Thinking

1. The complaint is not valid. 20,000 Hz is beyond the range of human hearing.

2. Answers will vary. Sample answer: This could result from "dead spots" inside the coliseum. The sound waves are interfering destructively with each other as they overlap.

3. Answers will vary. Sample answer: Lining the walls with soft substances would absorb the sound waves. Irregularly shaped foam-rubber blocks could be placed throughout the arena to scatter the sound waves.

4. Answers will vary. Sample answer: In a woodwind instrument, the pitch depends in part on the length of the air column. The longer the column, the lower the pitch. Mr. Mozart could lengthen the air column of his tuba.

5. The sound waves from the horn of the stationary car are compressed as the patrol car approaches and lengthened as the patrol car passes. This causes the sound of the horn to change pitch. This is called the Doppler effect.

Section Quizzes

SECTION: WHAT IS SOUND?

1. A	**5.** C
2. C	**6.** A
3. B	**7.** B
4. A	

SECTION: PROPERTIES OF SOUND

1. D	**6.** J
2. A	**7.** I
3. C	**8.** B
4. G	**9.** F
5. E	**10.** H

SECTION: INTERACTIONS OF SOUND WAVES

1. I	**6.** A
2. J	**7.** E
3. D	**8.** G
4. B	**9.** C
5. H	**10.** F

SECTION: SOUND QUALITY

1. C	**4.** A
2. B	**5.** D
3. D	

Chapter Test A

1. A	**14.** C
2. B	**15.** A
3. D	**16.** D
4. C	**17.** E
5. A	**18.** J
6. A	**19.** F
7. C	**20.** B
8. A	**21.** C
9. A	**22.** A
10. I	**23.** D
11. H	**24.** D
12. B	**25.** A
13. G	

Chapter Test B

1. sound quality

2. loudness

Copyright © by Holt, Rinehart and Winston. All rights reserved.

3. ultrasonic
4. Doppler effect
5. pitch
6. D
7. C
8. D
9. B
10. A
11. An oscilloscope uses a microphone to convert the sound waves into an electric current. The oscilloscope then converts the current into a graph. The graph shows waves that have crests representing compressions, and troughs representing rarefactions.
12. Constructive interference occurs when the compressions of one wave overlap the compressions of another wave. This results in an increased amplitude, and it produces a louder sound. Destructive interference occurs when the compressions of one wave overlap the rarefactions of another wave. This decreases the amplitude, and produces a softer sound.
13. Ultrasonic waves are sent down into the water. They reflect off the objects and send echoes back to the surface, which are used to determine the location of the object.
14. Answers will vary. Sample answer: Jeremy could get an oscilloscope graph of the music. If it shows regular, repeating patterns, it would be considered music, and he would be right. However, if it shows a random mix of frequencies or pitches, then it would be considered noise and his parents would be correct. Since musical instruments are producing the sounds, the chances are that Jeremy is correct.
15. The string may not be taught so that it doesn't vibrate easily or it may be taught by touching something else, so that the vibrations are absorbed by the other object. She should tell them to stand so that the string is taught and straight between them and not touching anything.
16. Answers will vary. Sample answer: A box (the outer ear) has a piece of rubber (eardrum) stretched over the end. When the rubber vibrates, it causes a small, thick stick to vibrate (oval window) which causes a switch to turn (hairs in cochlea), so that a current starts up in a wire (electrical impulse in nerve) and lights a bulb (message is received in the brain).
17. **a.** middle portion; **b.** outer portion; **c.** vibrations; **d.** pinna; **e.** electrical signals; **f.** levers; **g.** brain; **h.** ear canal
18. Answers will vary. Sample answer: Because a soft whisper is 20 decibels and normal conversation is 60 decibels, the range of the human voice can be estimated to be between 15 decibels and 80 decibels.

Chapter Test C

1. A	12. C
2. B	13. A
3. C	14. pinna
4. A	15. decibel
5. D	16. noise
6. C	17. sonar
7. A	18. standing wave
8. F	19. oscilloscope
9. E	20. B
10. B	21. B
11. D	22. C

Standardized Test Preparation

READING
Passage 1
1. D
2. G
3. A

Passage 2
1. B
2. H
3. A

INTERPRETING GRAPHICS
1. A
2. D
3. B
4. F

MATH
1. C
2. H
3. B
4. H

Copyright © by Holt, Rinehart and Winston. All rights reserved.

Vocabulary Activity

1. Doppler effect
2. reflection
3. echo
4. echolocation
5. sound wave
6. sound quality
7. loudness, pitch
8. resonance
9. middle
10. inner
11. outer
12. interference
13. decibel
14. noise
15. sonic boom
16. standing wave
17. medium

F	B	O	E	F	F	E	C	T	I	I	Z	E	W
I	Q	U	A	L	I	T	Y	M	N	R	R	C	A
W	G	T	D	T	O	T	W	F	T	M	E	H	V
V	B	E	W	R	K	U	R	L	E	V	L	O	E
R	U	R	X	A	E	A	D	Z	R	S	P	L	B
X	E	M	E	D	I	U	M	N	F	U	P	O	O
E	L	N	Z	O	K	C	C	E	E	N	O	C	O
F	D	O	N	N	O	I	S	E	R	S	D	A	M
J	E	I	H	I	O	K	C	Z	E	K	S	T	I
C	C	S	O	U	N	D	Y	H	N	X	Y	I	O
M	I	N	R	R	E	F	L	E	C	T	I	O	N
C	B	N	E	M	I	D	D	L	E	T	Y	N	I
R	E	S	O	N	A	N	C	E	Q	U	I	A	O
P	L	O	E	S	T	A	N	D	I	N	G	P	G

SciLinks Activity

1. Answers will vary. Sample answer: **a.** Most bats produce sounds with their voice box, but some click their tongues. **b.** Echolocation calls vary in frequency from 20 to 200 Hz. **c.** Echolocation calls are characterized by their frequency, their decibel level, and their length (in milliseconds). **d.** Most bat calls are very complex, and a combination of constant and changing frequencies.
2. Answers will vary, but should include the facts listed in question 1.

Copyright © by Holt, Rinehart and Winston. All rights reserved.

Lesson Plan

Section: What Is Sound?

Pacing

Regular Schedule: **with lab(s):** N/A   **without lab(s):** 1 day

Block Schedule: **with lab(s):** N/A   **without lab(s):** 0.5 day

Objectives

1. Describe how vibrations cause sound.

2. Explain how sound is transmitted through a medium.

3. Explain how the human ear works, and identify its parts.

4. Identify ways to protect your hearing.

National Science Education Standards Covered

SAI 1: Abilities necessary to do scientific inquiry

SAI 2: Understandings about scientific inquiry

SPSP 1: Personal health

PS 3a: Energy is a property of many substances and is associated with heat, light, electricity, mechanical motion, sound, nuclei, and the nature of a chemical. Energy is transferred in many ways.

KEY

SE = Student Edition   **TE** = Teacher's Edition
CRF = Chapter Resource File

FOCUS *(5 minutes)*

_ **Chapter Starter Transparency** Use this transparency to introduce the chapter.

_ **Bellringer, TE** Have students describe times they have felt a sound.

_ **Bellringer Transparency** Use this transparency as students enter the classroom and find their seats.

_ **Reading Strategy, Prediction Guide, SE** Have students make predictions prior to reading the section. **(BASIC)**

MOTIVATE *(10 minutes)*

_ **Demonstration, Vibrations of Stereo Speakers, TE** Have students observe the vibration of the woofers of stereo speakers. **(GENERAL)**

_ **Teaching Transparency, Sounds from a Stereo Speaker** Use this transparency to explain the vibrations of the stereo speaker.

Copyright © by Holt, Rinehart and Winston. All rights reserved.

TEACH *(20 minutes)*

_ **Activity, Sounds in Your World, TE** Have students record the sounds they hear and identify them as pleasant or unpleasant. (**GENERAL**)

_ **Inclusion Strategies, TE** Use a drum to demonstrate the connection between vibrations and sound.

_ **Quick Lab, Good Vibrations, SE** Students strike a tuning fork on an eraser and observe the results in several ways. (**GENERAL**)

_ **Discussion, Sound in Space, TE** Discuss with students why some science fiction scenes in space with loud explosions are not scientifically accurate. (**GENERAL**)

_ **Group Activity, Sound Samples, TE** Have students record a variety of sounds and then compare and discuss them. (**GENERAL**)

_ **Activity, Diagrams of the Ear, TE** Have students draw and label the parts of the ear. (**BASIC**)

_ **Teaching Transparency, How the Human Ear Works** Use this transparency to explain how the ear works.

_ **Directed Reading A/B, CRF** These worksheets reinforce basic concepts and vocabulary presented in the lesson. (**BASIC/SPECIAL NEEDS**)

_ **Vocabulary and Section Summary, CRF** Students write definitions of key terms and read a summary of section content. (**GENERAL**)

CLOSE *(10 minutes)*

_ **Reteaching, Retracing the Process of Sound and Hearing, TE** Have students draw sketches of sound production and travel and what happens when sound reaches the ear. (**BASIC**)

_ **Homework, Hearing Aids, TE** Have students research hearing aids. (**GENERAL**)

_ **Section Review, SE** Students answer end-of-section vocabulary, key ideas, critical thinking, and interpreting graphics questions. (**GENERAL**)

_ **Section Quiz, CRF** Students answer 8 objective questions about sound. (**GENERAL**)

_ **Quiz, TE** Students answer 2 questions about sound. (**GENERAL**)

_ **Alternative Assessment, Hearing Problem, TE** Students write fictional letters about a hearing problem in the workplace. (**GENERAL**)

Copyright © by Holt, Rinehart and Winston. All rights reserved.

Lesson Plan

Section: Properties of Sound

Pacing

Regular Schedule: **with lab(s):** 2 days **without lab(s):** 1 day
Block Schedule: **with lab(s):** 1 day **without lab(s):** 0.5 day

Objectives

1. Compare the speed of sound in different media.
2. Explain how frequency and pitch are related.
3. Describe the Doppler effect, and give examples of it.
4. Explain how amplitude and loudness are related.
5. Describe how amplitude and frequency can be "seen" on an oscilloscope.

National Science Education Standards Covered

UCP 1: Systems, order, and organization

UCP 3: Change, constancy, and measurement

SAI 1: Abilities necessary to do scientific inquiry

SAI 2: Understandings about scientific inquiry

PS 3a: Energy is a property of many substances and is associated with heat, light, electricity, mechanical motion, sound, nuclei, and the nature of a chemical. Energy is transferred in many ways.

KEY
SE = Student Edition **TE** = Teacher's Edition
CRF = Chapter Resource File

FOCUS (*5 minutes*)

_ **Bellringer, TE** Have students answer a riddle about sound traveling through space.

_ **Bellringer Transparency** Use this transparency as students enter the classroom and find their seats.

MOTIVATE (*10 minutes*)

_ **Activity, Paper Cup Phones, TE** Have teams of students make and use paper cup phones. (**GENERAL**)

Copyright © by Holt, Rinehart and Winston. All rights reserved.

TEACH *(65 minutes)*

_ **Reading Strategy, Reading Organizer, SE** Have students create an outline of the section as they read it. (**BASIC**)

_ **Teaching Transparency, Frequency and Pitch** Use this transparency to explain the relationship between frequency and pitch.

_ **Connection Activity Math, Speed of Sound in Steel, TE** Students estimate how long it will take a sound to travel through a steel railing. (**GENERAL**)

_ **Activity, Doppler Diagram, TE** Have students draw a diagram to illustrate the Doppler effect. (**BASIC**)

_ **Demonstration, The Doppler Effect In Action, TE** Swing a noisemaker around on a string to illustrate the Doppler effect. (**GENERAL**)

_ **Reinforcement, Doppler Dan's Dump Truck, CRF** This worksheet reinforces key concepts in the chapter. (**BASIC**)

_ **Connection to Real World, Loud Music, TE** Provide students with information about loud sounds that can damage hearing. (**GENERAL**)

_ **Quick Lab, Sounding Board, SE** Students use a vibrating ruler to explore the connection between amplitude and volume and wavelength and pitch. (**GENERAL**)

_ **Chapter Lab, Easy Listening, SE** Students measure their classmates' ability to detect sounds of different pitches at different distances. (**GENERAL**)

_ **Research, TE** Have students research a topic from the chapter and relate it to their lives. (**GENERAL**)

_ **Using the Graph, TE** Students use the graph in the text to answer questions about the range of frequencies that animals and humans can hear. (**GENERAL**)

_ **Directed Reading A/B, CRF** These worksheets reinforce basic concepts and vocabulary presented in the lesson. (**BASIC/SPECIAL NEEDS**)

_ **Vocabulary and Section Summary, CRF** Students write definitions of key terms and read a summary of section content. (**GENERAL**)

CLOSE *(10 minutes)*

_ **Reteaching, Sound Relationships, TE** Have students make connections between the terms "frequency," "amplitude," "loudness," and "pitch." (**BASIC**)

_ **Section Review, SE** Students answer end-of-section vocabulary, key ideas, math, and critical thinking questions. (**GENERAL**)

_ **Section Quiz, CRF** Students answer 10 objective questions about sound. (**GENERAL**)

_ **Quiz, TE** Students answer 2 questions about sound. (**GENERAL**)

_ **Alternative Assessment, TE** Students create a concept map showing the properties of sound. (**GENERAL**)

Copyright © by Holt, Rinehart and Winston. All rights reserved.

Lesson Plan

Section: Interactions of Sound Waves

Pacing

Regular Schedule:	**with lab(s):** N/A	**without lab(s):** 1 day
Block Schedule:	**with lab(s):** N/A	**without lab(s):** 0.5 day

Objectives

1. Explain how echoes are made, and describe their use in locating objects.

2. List examples of constructive and destructive interference of sound waves.

3. Explain what resonance is.

National Science Education Standards Covered

UCP 1: Systems, order, and organization

PS 3a: Energy is a property of many substances and is associated with heat, light, electricity, mechanical motion, sound, nuclei, and the nature of a chemical. Energy is transferred in many ways.

KEY

SE = Student Edition **TE** = Teacher's Edition
CRF = Chapter Resource File

FOCUS *(5 minutes)*

_ **Bellringer, TE** Have students answer questions about sound waves.

_ **Bellringer Transparency** Use this transparency as students enter the classroom and find their seats.

MOTIVATE *(10 minutes)*

_ **Demonstration, TE** Touch a tuning fork to water and have students explain why the water moves. (**GENERAL**)

TEACH *(20 minutes)*

_ **Reading Strategy, Paired Summarizing, SE** Have students utilize paired summarizing when reading the section. (**BASIC**)

_ **Connection Activity, Language Arts, The Power of Sound, TE** Have students write a story in which the plot depends on sound. (**GENERAL**)

_ **Inclusion Strategies, TE** Have students check various locations around the school to see whether sound waves reflect to create echoes.

Copyright © by Holt, Rinehart and Winston. All rights reserved.

- **SciLinks Activity, What Is Sound? SciLinks Code HSM1663, CRF** Students research Internet sources related to echolocation. (**GENERAL**)

- **Teaching Transparency, How Sonar Works** Use this transparency to explain sonar.

- **Teaching Transparency, Echolocation** Use this transparency to explain echolocation.

- **Connection Activity, Real World, TE** Have students research the sound transmission class ratings of building materials and design a house based on their research. (**GENERAL**)

- **Activity, Interference in Auditoriums, TE** Have students research how theaters, concert halls, and recording studios are designed and built to reduce destructive interference. (**ADVANCED**)

- **Research, TE** Have students research the history and development of sound recording. (**GENERAL**)

- **Activity, Advanced Learners, TE** Have students research active noise control and present their findings. (**ADVANCED**)

- **Critical Thinking, CRF** Ask students to fill out the worksheet about various aspects of sound. (**ADVANCED**)

- **Directed Reading A/B, CRF** These worksheets reinforce basic concepts and vocabulary presented in the lesson. (**BASIC/SPECIAL NEEDS**)

- **Vocabulary and Section Summary, CRF** Students write definitions of key terms and read a summary of section content. (**GENERAL**)

CLOSE *(10 minutes)*

- **Reteaching, Brainstorming Section Concepts, TE** Have students brainstorm the main ideas and subtopics covered in the section. (**BASIC**)

- **Section Review, SE** Students answer end-of-section vocabulary, key ideas, math, and critical thinking questions. (**GENERAL**)

- **Section Quiz, CRF** Students answer 10 objective questions about sound. (**GENERAL**)

- **Quiz, TE** Students answer 2 questions about sound. (**GENERAL**)

- **Alternative Assessment, Sound Stories, TE** Students write fictional stories about a strange phenomenon caused by the interaction of sound waves. (**GENERAL**)

Copyright © by Holt, Rinehart and Winston. All rights reserved.

Lesson Plan

Section: Sound Quality

Pacing

Regular Schedule:	**with lab(s):** N/A	**without lab(s):** 1 day
Block Schedule:	**with lab(s):** N/A	**without lab(s):** 0.5 day

Objectives

1. Explain why different instruments have different sound qualities.
2. Describe how each family of musical instruments produces sound.
3. Explain how noise is different from music.

National Science Education Standards Covered

UCP 5: Form and function

KEY

SE = Student Edition   **TE** = Teacher's Edition
CRF = Chapter Resource File

FOCUS *(5 minutes)*

_ **Bellringer, TE** Have students answer three questions about sound quality.

_ **Bellringer Transparency** Use this transparency as students enter the classroom and find their seats.

MOTIVATE *(10 minutes)*

_ **Demonstration, Musical Instruments, TE** Have volunteers demonstrate musical instruments and have students discuss the differences in the sound qualities. (**GENERAL**)

TEACH *(20 minutes)*

_ **Reading Strategy, Reading Organizer, SE** Have students make a table to compare the sounds of different instruments when reading the section. (**BASIC**)

_ **Activity, Making Models of Drums, TE** Have students make a model of a simple instrument. (**GENERAL**)

_ **Cultural Awareness, TE** Share with students information about the importance of drums in other cultures. (**GENERAL**)

_ **Debate, TE** Have students research and debate the advantages and disadvantages of adding runways to airports near residential areas. (**GENERAL**)

_ **Directed Reading A/B, CRF** These worksheets reinforce basic concepts and vocabulary presented in the lesson. (**BASIC/SPECIAL NEEDS**)

Copyright © by Holt, Rinehart and Winston. All rights reserved.

_ **Vocabulary and Section Summary, CRF** Students write definitions of key terms and read a summary of section content. (**GENERAL**)

CLOSE *(10 minutes)*

_ **Homework, The Sound of Music, TE** Have students write about a sound that is important to them. (**GENERAL**)

_ **Reteaching, Musical Instruments and Sound Quality, TE** Have students brainstorm the names of instruments in each family and describe what they have in common. (**BASIC**)

_ **Quiz, TE** Students answer 2 questions about sound. (**GENERAL**)

_ **Alternative Assessment, Instrument Diagram, TE** Students draw and label instruments from each family. (**GENERAL**)

_ **Section Review, SE** Students answer end-of-section vocabulary, key ideas, critical thinking, and interpreting graphics questions. (**GENERAL**)

_ **Section Quiz, CRF** Students answer 8 objective questions about sound. (**GENERAL**)

Copyright © by Holt, Rinehart and Winston. All rights reserved.

Lesson Plan

End of Chapter Review and Assessment

Pacing

Regular Schedule: **with lab(s):** N/A   **without lab(s):** 1 day

Block Schedule: **with lab(s):** N/A   **without lab(s):** 0.5 day

---

KEY
SE = Student Edition   **TE** = Teacher's Edition
CRF = Chapter Resource File

_ **Chapter Review, SE** Students answer end-of-chapter vocabulary, key ideas, critical thinking, and graphics questions. **(GENERAL)**

_ **Vocabulary Activity, CRF** Students review chapter vocabulary terms by completing a word search. **(GENERAL)**

_ **Concept Mapping Transparency** Use this graphic to help students review key concepts.

_ **Chapter Test A/B/C, CRF** Assign questions from the appropriate test for chapter assessment. **(GENERAL/ADVANCED/SPECIAL NEEDS)**

_ **Performance-Based Assessment, CRF** Assign this activity for general level assessment for the chapter. **(GENERAL)**

_ **Standardized Test Preparation, CRF** Students answer reading comprehension, math, and interpreting graphics questions in the format of a standardized test. **(GENERAL)**

_ **Test Generator, One-Stop Planner** Create a customized homework assignment, quiz, or test using the HRW Test Generator program. **(GENERAL)**

_ **CNN Video, CNN Presents Science in the News: Science, Technology & Society,** Segment 25, "Salmon Sound Barriers"

_ **CNN Video, CNN Presents Science in the News: Science, Technology & Society,** Segment 26, "Learning from Frog Ears"

Copyright © by Holt, Rinehart and Winston. All rights reserved.

The Nature of Sound

MULTIPLE CHOICE

1. Sound is created by
   a. the complete back-and-forth motion of objects.
   b. air particles slowing down.
   c. longitudinal waves.
   d. a substance through which sound can move.
   Answer: A   Difficulty: 1   Section: 1   Objective: 1

2. A substance through which a wave can travel is a
   a. longitudinal wave.   c. medium.
   b. vibration.   d. rarefaction.
   Answer: C   Difficulty: 1   Section: 1   Objective: 2

3. Which of the following is NOT a medium?
   a. a glass window   c. a metal fork
   b. a vacuum   d. the ocean
   Answer: B   Difficulty: 1   Section: 1   Objective: 2

4. One thing you can do to protect your hearing is to
   a. sit in the back of the room during a rock concert.
   b. use earphones when listening to the radio.
   c. eat a nutritious and balanced diet.
   d. sleep in a darkened room.
   Answer: A   Difficulty: 1   Section: 1   Objective: 4

5. Different instruments produce their own unique sound qualities because
   a. each one is played by a musician with a different amount of experience.
   b. each has several different pitches that mix together through resonance.
   c. each has several different pitches that mix together through interference.
   d. some produce fundamental frequencies and some produce overtones.
   Answer: C   Difficulty: 1   Section: 4   Objective: 1

6. What can a violinist do if one string is producing a sound that is too low?
   a. lengthen the string   c. attach the violin to an amplifier
   b. shorten the string   d. use a longer bow
   Answer: B   Difficulty: 1   Section: 4   Objective: 2

7. Which of the following sequences is correct?
   a. bridge vibrates; string vibrates; body of viola vibrates; resonance occurs
   b. body of viola vibrates; bridge vibrates; string vibrates; resonance occurs
   c. resonance occurs; bridge vibrates; string vibrates; body of viola vibrates
   d. string vibrates; bridge vibrates; body of viola vibrates; resonance occurs
   Answer: D   Difficulty: 1   Section: 4   Objective: 2

8. Which of the following will produce a noise?
   a. a car motor   c. a drum
   b. a guitar   d. a bass saxophone
   Answer: A   Difficulty: 1   Section: 4   Objective: 2

9. What produces a noise?
   a. a repeating pattern of frequencies   c. a random mix of volumes
   b. a repeating pattern of amplitudes   d. a random mix of frequencies
   Answer: D   Difficulty: 1   Section: 4   Objective: 3

Copyright © by Holt, Rinehart and Winston. All rights reserved.

10. The blending of pitches through interference produces an instrument's
    a. sound quality.
    b. amplitude.
    c. echoes.
    d. resonance.

    Answer: A   Difficulty: 1   Section: 3   Objective: 2

11. The amplitude of a sound's waves determines the sound's
    a. pitch.
    b. loudness.
    c. resonance.
    d. sound quality.

    Answer: B   Difficulty: 1   Section: 2   Objective: 4

12. Sounds with frequencies higher than 20,000 Hz
    a. result from standing waves.
    b. create destructive interference.
    c. are considered to be noise.
    d. are ultrasonic sounds.

    Answer: D   Difficulty: 1   Section: 2   Objective: 2

13. The motion of either the listener or the source of a sound causes
    a. resonance.
    b. shock waves.
    c. the Doppler effect.
    d. echolocation.

    Answer: C   Difficulty: 1   Section: 2   Objective: 3

14. The frequency of a sound wave determines
    a. the pitch of the sound.
    b. the loudness of the sound.
    c. the sound quality.
    d. the type of interference.

    Answer: A   Difficulty: 1   Section: 2   Objective: 2

15. Which statement about sound is NOT true?
    a. Air particles travel with sound waves.
    b. Sound waves cannot travel through a vacuum.
    c. Sound waves exist even if no one hears them.
    d. Air particles vibrate along the path of a sound wave.

    Answer: A   Difficulty: 2   Section: 1   Objective: 2

16. An echo is most likely to result when sound hits a surface that is
    a. bumpy and soft.
    b. smooth and soft.
    c. smooth and hard.
    d. bumpy and hard.

    Answer: C   Difficulty: 1   Section: 3   Objective: 1

17. The medium through which sound waves travel affects the
    a. speed of the sound.
    b. the amplitude of the waves.
    c. the number of waves per second.
    d. the sound quality.

    Answer: A   Difficulty: 1   Section: 1   Objective: 2

18. A person experiences a sonic boom when
    a. a shock wave reaches the ears.
    b. an airplane breaks the sound barrier.
    c. overtones are created.
    d. sound waves overlap by constructive interference.

    Answer: A   Difficulty: 1   Section: 3   Objective: 2

19. Which statement about sound is true?
    a. Air particles travel with sound waves.
    b. Sound waves can travel through a vacuum.
    c. Sound waves exist only if someone hears them.
    d. Air particles vibrate along the path of a sound wave.

    Answer: D   Difficulty: 1   Section: 1   Objective: 2

Copyright © by Holt, Rinehart and Winston. All rights reserved.

20. Sound waves are best reflected off which surfaces?
    a. bumpy, soft
    b. smooth, soft
    c. smooth, hard
    d. bumpy, hard

    Answer: C   Difficulty: 1   Section: 3   Objective: 1

21. The speed of a sound depends on
    a. its source.
    b. the force of its compressions.
    c. the number of waves per second.
    d. the medium through which it travels.

    Answer: D   Difficulty: 1   Section: 2   Objective: 1

22. For a sound wave to produce an echo, it must
    a. diffract around a small barrier.
    b. reflect off the surface of an object.
    c. have an ultrasonic frequency.
    d. have a very long wavelength.

    Answer: B   Difficulty: 1   Section: 3   Objective: 1

23. A sonic boom is experienced when
    a. a shock wave reaches an observer.
    b. a moving object breaks the sound barrier.
    c. a jet engine's thrust is suddenly increased.
    d. sound waves overlap by destructive interference.

    Answer: A   Difficulty: 1   Section: 3   Objective: 2

24. What does the mixing of pitches through interference produce?
    a. sound quality
    b. amplitude
    c. echoes
    d. resonance

    Answer: A   Difficulty: 1   Section: 4   Objective: 3

25. What does the amplitude of a sound's waves affect?
    a. pitch
    b. loudness
    c. resonance
    d. sound quality

    Answer: B   Difficulty: 1   Section: 2   Objective: 4

26. What does the motion of the source of a sound cause?
    a. resonance
    b. shock waves
    c. the Doppler effect
    d. echolocation

    Answer: C   Difficulty: 1   Section: 2   Objective: 3

27. What does the frequency of a sound wave affect?
    a. pitch
    b. loudness
    c. sound quality
    d. type of interference

    Answer: A   Difficulty: 1   Section: 2   Objective: 2

28. Which statement about sound waves is true?
    a. Air travels with them.
    b. They travel through a vacuum.
    c. They exist only if heard.
    d. They can mix.

    Answer: D   Difficulty: 1   Section: 3   Objective: 2

29. Which surface is the best reflector of sound?
    a. bumpy and soft
    b. smooth and soft
    c. smooth and hard
    d. bumpy and hard

    Answer: C   Difficulty: 1   Section: 3   Objective: 1

30. What does the medium through which sound waves travel affect?
    a. speed of the sound
    b. amplitude of the waves
    c. number of waves per second
    d. sound quality

    Answer: A   Difficulty: 1   Section: 1   Objective: 2

Copyright © by Holt, Rinehart and Winston. All rights reserved.

31. Which of the following represents the correct sequence of events?
    a. a drum vibrates; air particles near a drum are pushed closer together and then become less crowded; compressions and rarefactions travel away from a drum; hair cells in the cochlea bend; the hammer vibrates
    b. hair cells in the cochlea bend; the hammer vibrates; a drum vibrates; air particles near a drum are pushed closer together and then become less crowded; compressions and rarefactions travel away from a drum
    c. air particles near a drum are pushed closer together and then become less crowded; compressions and rarefactions travel away from a drum; a drum vibrates; hair cells in the cochlea bend; the hammer vibrates
    d. a drum vibrates; air particles near a drum are pushed closer together and then become less crowded; compressions and rarefactions travel away from the drum; the hammer vibrates; hair cells in the cochlea bend

    Answer: C   Difficulty: 4   Section: 1   Objective: 1, 2, 3

32. Which of the following represents the correct sequence of events?
    a. sound waves pass from an area of hot air to an area of cold air; the speed of the sound waves slows; sound waves travel from air into water; the speed of the sound waves increases
    b. sound waves pass from an area of hot air to an area of cold air; the speed of the sound waves increases; sound waves travel from air into water; the speed of the sound waves increases
    c. sound waves pass from an area of hot air to an area of cold air; the speed of the sound waves increases; sound waves travel from air into water; the speed of the sound waves slows
    d. sound waves pass from an area of hot air to an area of cold air; the speed of the sound waves slows; sound waves travel from air into water; the speed of the sound waves slows

    Answer: D   Difficulty: 4   Section: 2   Objective: 1

33. Dwayne's violin is playing out of tune. Most of the notes are too low. What should he do?
    a. shorten the bow
    b. shorten the strings
    c. get thicker strings
    d. get a new guitar

    Answer: B   Difficulty: 4   Section: 4   Objective: 2

33. In which situation does a pilot have to travel the fastest in order to break the sound barrier?
    a. at 4000 m above sea level
    b. at 12,000 m above sea level
    c. in outer space
    d. at the edge of the shock wave

    Answer: B   Difficulty: 3   Section: 2, 3   Objective: 1, 2

34. Which person will experience what happens to sounds due to the Doppler effect?
    a. a father pushing a laughing toddler on a swing
    b. two friends riding bicycles side-by-side and talking
    c. a boy sitting and watching television
    d. a girl running and listening to her radio through earphones

    Answer: A   Difficulty: 3   Section: 2   Objective: 3

35. Which of the following people is most likely to suffer from tinnitus?
    a. an elderly person
    b. a former rock star
    c. a young child
    d. a worker in a quiet office

    Answer: B   Difficulty: 3   Section: 1   Objective: 4

36. Which sound has the highest pitch?
    a. one with 156 Hz
    b. one with 258 Hz
    c. one with 14 dB
    d. one with 563 dB

    Answer: B   Difficulty: 3   Section: 2   Objective: 2

Copyright © by Holt, Rinehart and Winston. All rights reserved.

37. Which sound has air particles that vibrate across the greatest distance?
    a. one with 156 Hz
    b. one with 258 Hz
    c. one with 14 dB
    d. one with 563 dB

    Answer: D   Difficulty: 3   Section: 2   Objective: 4

38. Which of the following could NOT be considered a percussion instrument?
    a. two sticks being knocked together
    b. a piece of grass held between the thumbs and blown on
    c. wind chimes blowing in the wind
    d. an oatmeal container filled with beans and shaken

    Answer: B   Difficulty: 3   Section: 4   Objective: 3

39. A person who cannot hear high-pitched sounds well is most likely NOT to hear
    a. the fundamental overtone.
    b. the first overtone.
    c. the second overtone.
    d. the third overtone.

    Answer: D   Difficulty: 3   Section: 3   Objective: 2

40. The sound quality of Pete's acoustic guitar seems to be suffering. He is suspicious that his little brother
    a. put his stuffed bear inside it.
    b. wrote his name on the guitar.
    c. put tape on the back of the guitar.
    d. played his guitar.

    Answer: A   Difficulty: 3   Section: 3   Objective: 3

41. Roberto came home and discovered his bedroom window broken. It is the only window on the north side of the house. Roberto asked around, but no one had been playing in the yard. What question should Roberto ask his neighbors?
    a. Did you see any bats?
    b. Did you see an airplane?
    c. Did you hear ultrasonic sounds?
    d. Did you hear 20 Db sounds?

    Answer: B   Difficulty: 3   Section: 3   Objective: 2

COMPLETION

Use the terms from the following list to complete the sentences below.

echolocation
sound quality
loudness
resonance
Doppler effect
pitch
ultrasonic

42. An instrument's ______________________ comes from the blending of pitches through interference.

    Answer: sound quality
                    Difficulty: 1   Section: 4   Objective: 2

43. The amplitude of a sound's waves determines its ______________________.

    Answer: loudness   Difficulty: 1   Section: 2   Objective: 5

44. Sounds with frequencies higher than 20,000 Hz are ______________________.

    Answer: ultrasonic   Difficulty: 1   Section: 2   Objective: 2

45. The motion of either the listener or the source of a sound causes the

    ______________________.

    Answer: Doppler effect
                    Difficulty: 1   Section: 2   Objective: 3

46. The frequency of the sound wave determines its ______________________.

    Answer: pitch   Difficulty: 1   Section: 2   Objective: 2

Copyright © by Holt, Rinehart and Winston. All rights reserved.

Use the terms from the following list to complete the sentences below.

pinna	oscilloscope
decibel	noise
standing wave	sonar

47. Sound is directed to the ear canal by the ___________________.
    Answer: pinna   Difficulty: 1   Section: 1   Objective: 3

48. The unit for measuring the loudness of sound is the ___________________.
    Answer: decibel   Difficulty: 1   Section: 2   Objective: 4

49. A sound with a random mixture of frequencies is ___________________.
    Answer: noise   Difficulty: 1   Section: 4   Objective: 3

50. Electronic echolocation, or ___________________, is used to find things underwater.
    Answer: sonar   Difficulty: 1   Section: 3   Objective: 1

51. Part of a(n) ___________________ has a large amplitude due to interference.
    Answer: standing wave
                           Difficulty: 1   Section: 3   Objective: 2

52. A graph of a sound can be made with a(n) ___________________.
    Answer: oscilloscope   Difficulty: 1   Section: 2   Objective: 5

SHORT ANSWER

53. How is an oscilloscope used to "see" sound waves?
    Answer:
    An oscilloscope uses a microphone to convert the sound waves into an electric current.
    The oscilloscope then converts the current into a graph. The graph shows waves that
    have crests representing compressions, and troughs representing rarefactions.
    Difficulty: 2   Section: 2   Objective: 5

54. Explain the difference between constructive interference and destructive interference.
    Answer:
    Constructive interference occurs when the compressions of one wave overlap the
    compressions of another wave. This results in an increased amplitude, and it produces
    a louder sound. Destructive interference occurs when the compressions of one wave
    overlap the rarefactions of another wave. This decreases the amplitude, and produces
    a softer sound.
    Difficulty: 3   Section: 3   Objective: 2

55. How are echoes used to locate underwater objects?
    Answer:
    Ultrasonic waves are sent down into the water. They reflect off the objects and send
    echoes back to the surface, which are used to determine the location of the object.
    Difficulty: 2   Section: 3   Objective: 1

56. Name the three bones in the ear that act as levers.
    Answer: hammer, stirrup, anvil
    Difficulty: 1   Section: 1   Objective: 3

57. What is necessary for sound to travel from its source to a listener?
    Answer: a medium through which the sound waves can travel
    Difficulty: 2   Section: 1   Objective: 2

58. Name three properties of sound.
    Answer: speed, pitch, and loudness
    Difficulty: 2   Section: 2   Objective: 1, 2, 4

Copyright © by Holt, Rinehart and Winston. All rights reserved.

59. Explain how a person can observe the Doppler effect.
    Answer:
    When a loud noise is moving toward or away from a listener, the sound appears to change pitch because the sound waves are moving closer together or farther apart relative to the listener's position.
    Difficulty: 2   Section: 2   Objective: 3

60. Why does everything seem so quiet after a snowfall?
    Answer: Snow does not reflect sound waves, it absorbs them.
    Difficulty: 3   Section: 3   Objective: 1

61. Have you ever sung in the shower? Why does your voice sound so much better there?
    Answer:
    The hard, smooth walls of the shower reflect sound waves, and the interactions of the waves make your voice sound fuller.
    Difficulty: 3   Section: 3   Objective: 1, 2

62. What is sound quality?
    Answer: the result of several pitches blending together through interference
    Difficulty: 2   Section: 4   Objective: 1

63. How does noise differ from music?
    Answer:
    Music contains repeating melodic patterns. It is pleasant to listen to. Noise has a complex sound wave with no pattern and is not pleasing to the ear.
    Difficulty: 2   Section: 4   Objective: 3

64. Compare the rarefactions and compressions in the first and second overtones from a piano. Explain your comparison.
    Answer:
    In the first overtone, the rarefactions and compressions are farther apart than in the second overtone because the wavelengths are longer and the frequency is lower.
    Difficulty: 3   Section: 4   Objective: 1

65. How would a person's hearing be affected if the eardrum became loose and flabby?
    Answer:
    The eardrum would not vibrate as well, which would mean that it could not transfer the vibrations in sound waves to the middle ear. The person would not be able to hear very well, or even at all, depending on how loose the eardrum was.
    Difficulty: 3   Section: 1   Objective: 3

66 Stephanie's dad just got a new job in a very noisy factory. She is worried about him and wants to help. Why is she worried and what could she suggest to her dad to do?
    Answer:
    She is worried that the loud noises will damage his hearing. She could suggest to him to wear earplugs at work and to work as far from the noisy machines as he can.
    Difficulty: 3   Section: 1   Objective: 4

67. Talia plays the bass drum in the school marching band. She is worried that becoming tired during an upcoming parade will affect her playing. What effect might fatigue have and why?
    Answer:
    It is most likely that the volume will be affected because if she is tired she won't have as much energy to beat the drum hard. This will produce a softer sound.
    Difficulty: 3   Section: 2   Objective: 4

Copyright © by Holt, Rinehart and Winston. All rights reserved.

68. Compare the appearance of sound waves on an oscilloscope graph if one wave is louder and at a lower pitch than the other.

    Answer:
    The sound wave that is louder and lower will have higher and longer waves on the graph than the one that is softer and higher.

    Difficulty: 3   Section: 2   Objective: 5

69. The students in the drama club are putting on a science fiction play that takes place in outer space. The actors are in an airtight space ship. If their play is to be totally accurate, what will happen when the actors are walking in space? Why?

    Answer:
    No one will be able to hear them say anything because sound cannot travel through a vacuum.

    Difficulty: 3   Section: 1   Objective: 2

70. Ralph wants to try to get his drum to make a sound without touching it. What can he do?

    Answer:
    He can put another instrument, or a tuning fork, next to it, and have the instrument vibrate at the fundamental frequency of the drum. This will cause the drum to vibrate due to resonance.

    Difficulty: 3   Section: 3   Objective: 3

71. What are three ways that an oscilloscope changes sound waves?

    Answer:
    It changes a longitudinal wave into a transverse wave. It changes a sound wave into an electrical signal. It changes something you hear into something you see.

    Difficulty: 3   Section: 2   Objective: 5

72. At 10°C sound travels through air at 337 m/s. At 20°C sound travels through air at 343 m/s. How much farther will sound travel at 20°C in 10 seconds than at 10°C?
    Answer: 60 meters
    Difficulty: 3   Section: 1   Objective: 1

MATCHING

a. pitch	f. rarefactions
b. oscilloscope	g. decibels
c. Hertz	h. amplitude
d. medium	i. loudness
e. Doppler effect	j. ultrasonic

73. _____ speed of sound varies from one to another
    Answer: D   Difficulty: 1   Section: 2   Objective: 1
74. _____ how high or low a sound seems to be
    Answer: A   Difficulty: 1   Section: 2   Objective: 2
75. _____ units for expressing frequency
    Answer: C   Difficulty: 1   Section: 2   Objective: 2
76. _____ Sounds with 120 of these units can be painful.
    Answer: G   Difficulty: 1   Section: 2   Objective: 4
77. _____ causes a sound in front of a moving sound source to seem to have a higher pitch and frequency
    Answer: E   Difficulty: 1   Section: 2   Objective: 3
78. _____ sounds that have a frequency too high for people to hear
    Answer: J   Difficulty: 1   Section: 2   Objective: 2
79. _____ a measure of how well a sound can be heard
    Answer: I   Difficulty: 1   Section: 2   Objective: 4

Copyright © by Holt, Rinehart and Winston. All rights reserved.

80. ____ used to graph representations of sound wave

    Answer: B   Difficulty: 1   Section: 2   Objective: 5

81. ____ represented by the troughs on a graph from an oscilloscope

    Answer: F   Difficulty: 1   Section: 2   Objective: 5

82. ____ When it is larger, the sound is louder.

    Answer: H   Difficulty: 1   Section: 2   Objective: 4

a. echo	f. resonance
b. echolocation	g. destructive
c. interference	h. constructive
d. sonic boom	i. sonar
e. standing wave	j. ultrasonography

83. ____ technology that uses echoes to locate objects

    Answer: I   Difficulty: 1   Section: 3   Objective: 1

84. ____ a medical procedure used to check the development of an unborn baby in a mother's body

    Answer: J   Difficulty: 1   Section: 3   Objective: 1

85. ____ explosive sound heard when shock waves arrive at a person's ears

    Answer: D   Difficulty: 1   Section: 3   Objective: 2

86. ____ process in which a dolphin uses reflected waves to determine how far away objects are

    Answer: B   Difficulty: 1   Section: 3   Objective: 1

87. ____ interference used by a band when several instruments play the same note

    Answer: H   Difficulty: 1   Section: 3   Objective: 2

88. ____ a reflected sound wave

    Answer: A   Difficulty: 1   Section: 3   Objective: 1

89. ____ formed at a fundamental frequency or an overtone

    Answer: E   Difficulty: 1   Section: 3   Objective: 3

90. ____ interference that may cause people not to hear sounds in an auditorium

    Answer: G   Difficulty: 1   Section: 3   Objective: 2

91. ____ when two or more waves combine to form a single wave

    Answer: C   Difficulty: 1   Section: 3   Objective: 2

92. ____ occurs when a vibrating tuning fork causes a rubber band to vibrate

    Answer: F   Difficulty: 1   Section: 3   Objective: 3

a. sound wave	f. overtones
b. echolocation	g. interference
c. resonance	h. woodwind instrument
d. standing wave	i. percussion instrument
e. decibel	j. tinnitus

93. ____ vibrates when struck

    Answer: I   Difficulty: 1   Section: 4   Objective: 1

94. ____ vibration causes standing waves inside its air column

    Answer: H   Difficulty: 1   Section: 4   Objective: 1

95. ____ the use of reflected sound waves to find food or other objects

    Answer: B   Difficulty: 1   Section: 3   Objective: 1

96 ____ occurs when two instruments play the same note

    Answer: G   Difficulty: 1   Section: 3   Objective: 1

97. ____ the sound produced by one object causes another object to vibrate

    Answer: C   Difficulty: 1   Section: 3   Objective: 3

98. ____ longitudinal wave caused by vibrations and carried through a medium

    Answer: A   Difficulty: 1   Section: 1   Objective: 2

Copyright © by Holt, Rinehart and Winston. All rights reserved.

99. ____ a pattern of vibration that looks like a wave is at rest
    Answer: D   Difficulty: 1   Section: 3   Objective: 2
100. ____ unit for measuring loudness
    Answer: E   Difficulty: 1   Section: 2   Objective: 4
101. ____ results from long-term exposure to loud sounds
    Answer: J   Difficulty: 1   Section: 1   Objective: 4
102. ____ frequencies two or more times the fundamental frequency
    Answer: F   Difficulty: 1   Section: 3   Objective: 2

     a. cochlea   d. interference
     b. echolocation   e. woodwind instrument
     c. resonance   f. percussion instrument

103. ____ A larger instrument has a lower sound.
    Answer: F   Difficulty: 1   Section: 4   Objective: 1
104. ____ Standing waves form inside its air column.
    Answer: E   Difficulty: 1   Section: 4   Objective: 1
105. ____ It is the use of reflected sound waves to find objects.
    Answer: B   Difficulty: 1   Section: 3   Objective: 1
106. ____ It occurs when two or more waves overlap.
    Answer: D   Difficulty: 1   Section: 3   Objective: 2
107. ____ The sound produced by one object causes another object to vibrate.
    Answer: C   Difficulty: 1   Section: 3   Objective: 3
108. ____ A part of the ear that contains a liquid.
    Answer: A   Difficulty: 1   Section: 1   Objective: 3

ESSAY

109. Jeremy's parents do not like the music that he listens to. They call it noise and tell him to turn it down or turn it off. Jeremy wants to prove to his parents that it really is music. What could he do? Explain how his results might prove him or his parents correct.
    Answer:
    Jeremy could get an oscilloscope graph of the music. If it shows regular, repeating patterns, it would be considered music, and he would be right. However, if it shows a random mix of frequencies or pitches, then it would be considered noise and his parents would be correct. Since musical instruments are producing the sounds, the chances are that Jeremy is correct.
    Difficulty: 3   Section: 2   Objective: 4

110. Maria's little brother and sister have made a tin-can telephone, but they can't hear each other with it. What might be the problem? What tips should Maria give them so their toy will work better?
    Answer:
    The string may not be taught so that it doesn't vibrate easily or it may be taught by touching something else, so that the vibrations are absorbed by the other object. She should tell them to stand so that the string is taught and straight between them and not touching anything.
    Difficulty: 3   Section: 1   Objective: 2

111. For a science fair project, Terri wants to make a model to show how the ear detects sounds. What might her model look like, and how might it work?
    Answer:
    Sample answer. A box (the outer ear) has a piece of rubber (eardrum) stretched over the end. When the rubber vibrates, it causes a small, thick stick to vibrate (oval window) which causes a switch to turn (hairs in cochlea), so that a current starts up in a wire (electrical impulse in nerve) and lights a bulb (message is received in the brain).
    Difficulty: 3   Section: 1   Objective: 3

Copyright © by Holt, Rinehart and Winston. All rights reserved.

112. A group of friends went to a rock concert, but they couldn't all sit together. Some sat on one side of the auditorium, and others sat on the other side. A few sat near the front and some sat near the back. Afterward, they had an argument about the music. Some thought it was too loud, others said it was just right, and still others said that at times they could hardly hear. Why do you think the friends disagreed? Explain your answer.

Answer:

It could have been a matter of opinion, but it also could have been a matter of science. If the auditorium was not well designed, sound waves may have reflected off the walls, causing destructive interference with the sound waves from the stage resulting in the sounds that were softer. This may have caused some people not to hear well. The volume of the music could be checked by determining the amplitude of the waves and measuring the decibel level to determine whether or not the volume was above what is comfortable for the human ear.

Difficulty: 3   Section: 2, 3   Objective: 4, 2

113. A scientist discovers a new kind of animal living deep in a cave. It has four legs and fur, and is blind from birth. The scientist's hypothesis is that the animal makes use of echolocation to locate and capture food. Evaluate the scientist's hypothesis and explain how the scientist could obtain data to support it.

Answer:

The hypothesis is probably correct because echolocation is a way animals find objects without seeing. To test the hypothesis, the scientist could use an oscilloscope to record sound waves in the cave near the animals, making sure that the oscilloscope can record very high frequency sound waves. If the oscilloscope records high frequency sound waves coming from the animal and then being reflected back to it, this would show that the animal uses echolocation.

Difficulty: 3   Section: 3   Objective: 1

114. Imagine that you have been hired to design an auditorium. It will be used for concerts, lectures, and many other events. Describe how you will design the auditorium and why you will do it this way.

Answer:

The walls of the auditorium will have soft, rough materials to absorb sound waves and irregular shapes that will scatter the sound. This will help prevent sound waves being reflected back to the stage and causing destructive interference with the sounds coming from the stage.

Difficulty: 3   Section: 3   Objective: 2

115. Imagine that you are a composer and you have been asked to write a piece of music that is mostly at a very high pitch. What types of instruments would you use?

Answer:

I would use string instruments with very thin, short strings. I would use wind instruments with a very short air column, and percussion instruments that are very small.

Difficulty: 3   Section: 4   Objective: 3

Copyright © by Holt, Rinehart and Winston. All rights reserved.

INTERPRETING GRAPHICS

Use the image below to answer the following questions.

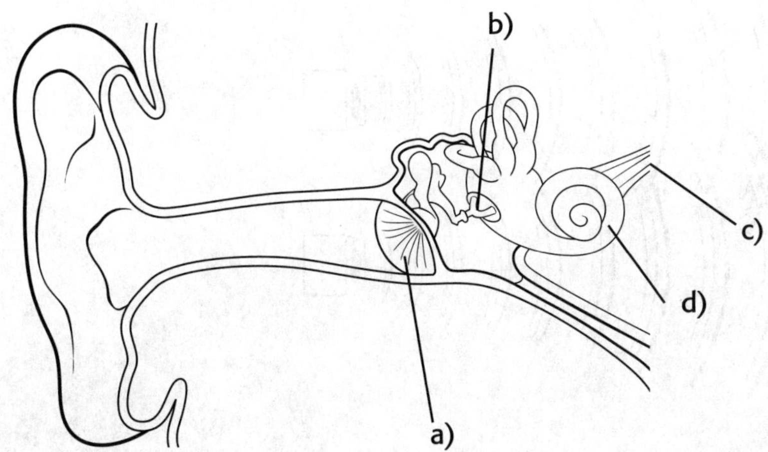

116. ____ Which part of the ear increases the size of the vibrations?
    Answer: C   Difficulty: 2   Section: 1   Objective: 3

117. ____ Which part of the ear do sound waves have to pass through in order to get from the outer ear to the middle ear?
    Answer: A   Difficulty: 2   Section: 1   Objective: 3

118. ____ Which part of the ear contains a liquid and tiny hairs?
    Answer: B   Difficulty: 2   Section: 1   Objective: 3

Use the image below to answer the following questions.

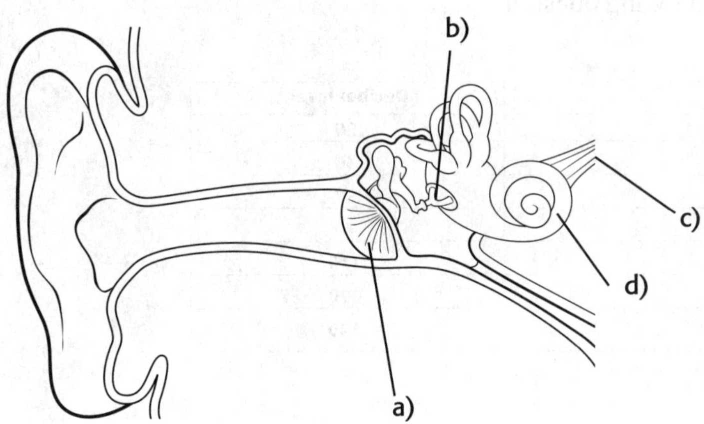

119. ____ The vibrating stirrup causes the oval window to vibrate.
    Answer: B   Difficulty: 2   Section: 1   Objective: 3

120. ____ Electrical signals are sent to the brain due to stimulation of nerves by bending hair cells.
    Answer: C   Difficulty: 2   Section: 1   Objective: 3

121. ____ Sound waves cause the eardrum to vibrate.
    Answer: A   Difficulty: 2   Section: 1   Objective: 3

122. ____ Movement of liquid inside cochlea causes hair cells to bend.
    Answer: D   Difficulty: 2   Section: 1   Objective: 3

Copyright © by Holt, Rinehart and Winston. All rights reserved.

Use the image below to answer the following questions.

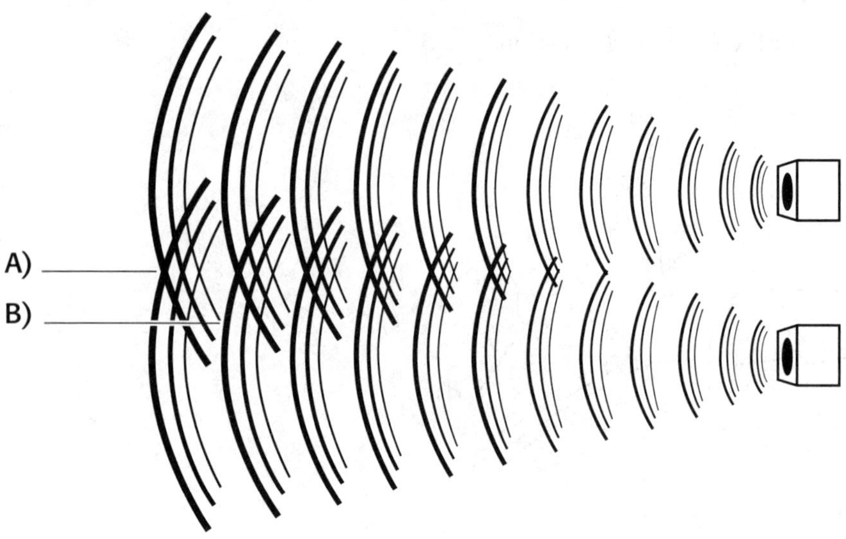

123. _____ Look at the diagram. What happens at point A?
   a. Compressions of one wave overlap rarefactions of another to create a softer sound.
   b. Compressions of one wave overlap rarefactions of another to create a louder sound.
   c. Compressions of one wave overlap compressions of another to create a softer sound.
   d. Compressions of one wave overlap compressions of another to create a louder sound.
   Answer: D   Difficulty: 2   Section: 3   Objective: 2

124. _____ Look at the diagram. What happens at point B?
   a. The amplitude is decreased.   c. The frequency is increased.
   b. The amplitude is increased.   d. The frequency is decreased.
   Answer: A   Difficulty: 2   Section: 3   Objective: 2

Use the chart below to answer the following question.

Sound	Decibel level
a soft whisper	20
leaves rustling	30
normal conversation	60
automobile accelerating	70
motorcycle engine	110
rock concert	120
jet plane taking off	140

125. What is a reasonable estimate of the range of decibel levels the human voice can produce?
   Answer:
      Answers will vary. Sample answer: Because a soft whisper is 20 decibels and normal conversation is 60 decibels, the range of the human voice can be estimated to be between 15 decibels and 80 decibels.
   Difficulty: 3   Section: 2   Objective: 4

Copyright © by Holt, Rinehart and Winston. All rights reserved.

Use the image below to answer the following questions.

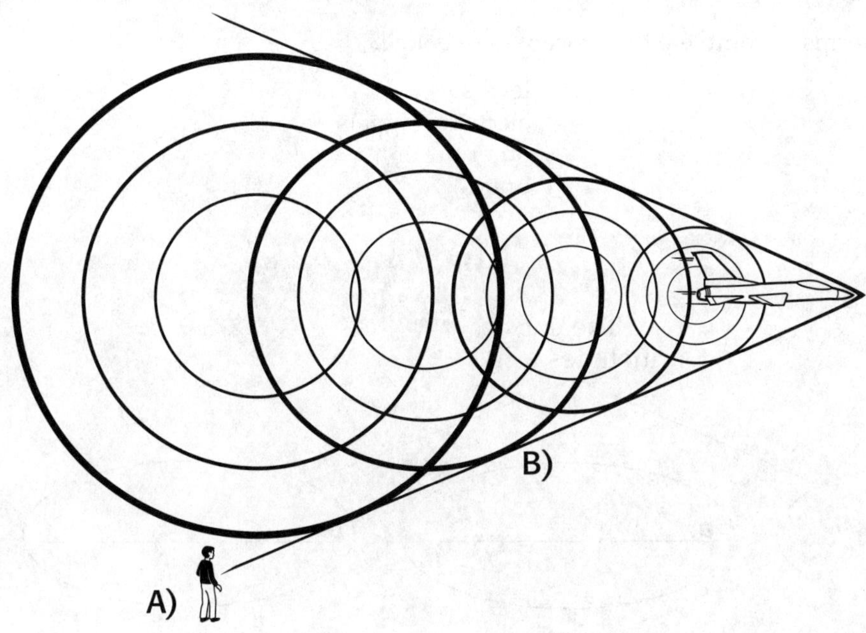

126. Look at the diagram. When does the person at point A hear the sonic boom?
  a. when the jet breaks the sound barrier
  b. when the shock waves reach the person
  c. when the jet travels faster than sound
  d. when the sonic boom occurs
  Answer: B   Difficulty: 3   Section: 3   Objective: 2

127. Look at the diagram. What happens at point B?
  a. deconstructive interference   c. sonic boom is produced
  b. shock wave is produced   d. supersonic speeds
  Answer: B   Difficulty: 3   Section: 3   Objective: 2

128. Look at the diagram. What do the circles show?
  a. sonic booms   c. sound waves
  b. shock waves   d. supersonic speeds
  Answer: C   Difficulty: 3   Section: 3   Objective: 2

Copyright © by Holt, Rinehart and Winston. All rights reserved.

CONCEPT MAPPING

129. Use the following terms to complete the concept map below:

middle portion	levers
ear canal	electrical signals
pinna	outer portion
vibrations	brain

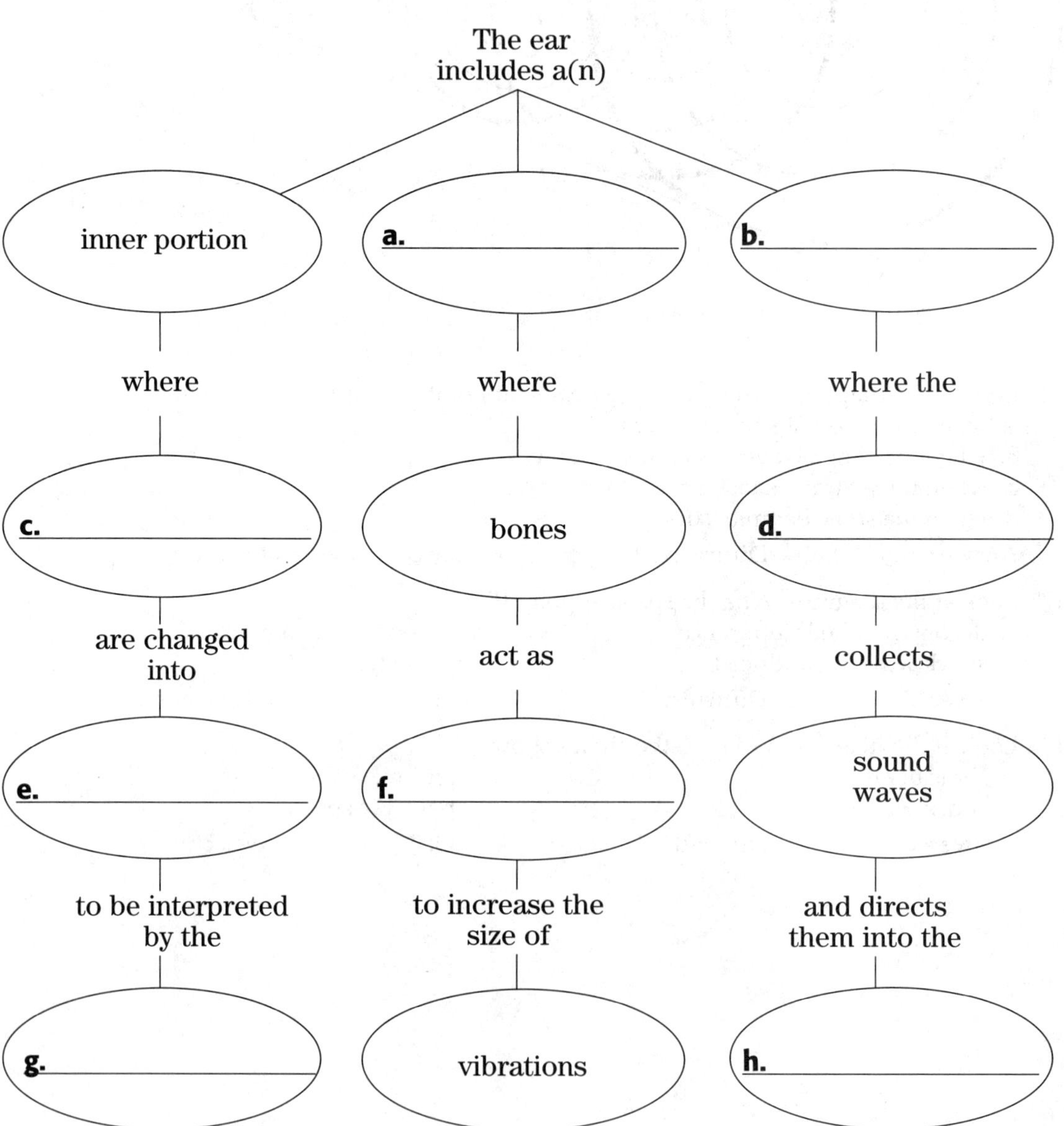

Answer:
   a. middle portion; b. outer portion; c. vibrations; d. pinna; e. electrical signals; f. levers;
   g. brain; h. ear canal

Difficulty: 3   Section: 1   Objective: 3

Copyright © by Holt, Rinehart and Winston. All rights reserved.

9997282388   2 3 4 5 6